Cambridge Elements

Elements in Philosophy of Law
edited by
George Pavlakos
University of Glasgow
Gerald J. Postema
University of North Carolina at Chapel Hill
Kenneth M. Ehrenberg
University of Surrey

Associate Editor
Sally Zhu
University of Sheffield

THE IMPASSE OF CONSTITUTIONAL RIGHTS

Jacob Weinrib
Queen's University

CAMBRIDGE
UNIVERSITY PRESS

Shaftesbury Road, Cambridge CB2 8EA, United Kingdom

One Liberty Plaza, 20th Floor, New York, NY 10006, USA

477 Williamstown Road, Port Melbourne, VIC 3207, Australia

314–321, 3rd Floor, Plot 3, Splendor Forum, Jasola District Centre,
New Delhi – 110025, India

103 Penang Road, #05–06/07, Visioncrest Commercial, Singapore 238467

Cambridge University Press is part of Cambridge University Press & Assessment,
a department of the University of Cambridge.

We share the University's mission to contribute to society through the pursuit
of education, learning and research at the highest international levels of excellence.

www.cambridge.org
Information on this title: www.cambridge.org/9781009517768

DOI: 10.1017/9781009010078

© Jacob Weinrib 2025

This publication is in copyright. Subject to statutory exception and to the provisions
of relevant collective licensing agreements, no reproduction of any part may take
place without the written permission of Cambridge University Press & Assessment.

When citing this work, please include a reference to the DOI 10.1017/9781009010078

First published 2025

A catalogue record for this publication is available from the British Library

ISBN 978-1-009-51776-8 Hardback
ISBN 978-1-009-00964-5 Paperback
ISSN 2631-5815 (online)
ISSN 2631-5807 (print)

Cambridge University Press & Assessment has no responsibility for the persistence
or accuracy of URLs for external or third-party internet websites referred to in this
publication and does not guarantee that any content on such websites is, or will
remain, accurate or appropriate.

The Impasse of Constitutional Rights

Elements in Philosophy of Law

DOI: 10.1017/9781009010078
First published online: March 2025

Jacob Weinrib
Queen's University
Author for correspondence: Jacob Weinrib, jacob.weinrib@queensu.ca

Abstract: Constitutional rights are often seen as invitations to engage in all things considered moral reasoning about how public authorities should act. *The Impasse of Constitutional Rights* challenges this widely accepted view by showing that it generates an irresolvable deadlock between rival theories of constitutional rights that share the same defects. This Element develops the alternative idea that rights-based constitutional order has its own distinctive moral project, which consists in rendering public authority accountable to the inherent rights of each legal subject. Taking this project seriously requires reconceiving the basic building blocks of rights-based constitutional order: justification, purposive interpretation, and proportionality. The resulting account both escapes the impasse to which the leading contemporary theories of constitutional rights succumb and expounds the normative connection between rights-based constitutional order and its most fundamental doctrines.

Keywords: constitutional rights, constitutional interpretation, proportionality, limitation clauses, justification

© Jacob Weinrib 2025
ISBNs: 9781009517768 (HB), 9781009009645 (PB), 9781009010078 (OC)
ISSNs: 2631-5815 (online), 2631-5807 (print)

Contents

Preface   1

1 The Impasse   4

2 Constitutional Justification   23

3 The Scope of Rights   33

4 The Strength of Rights   48

5 Conclusion   71

References   73

The Impasse of Constitutional Rights 1

> The common assumption is once again the notion (not so much articulated as put into practice) that the constitution in principle gives the interpreter a free choice of the different theories; no theory is ruled out, and the interpretation of the fundamental rights can be based on any of them, whether generally or on a case-by-case basis. It is precisely this assumption that needs to be challenged critically.
> —Ernst-Wolfgang Böckenförde (2016), p. 286.

Preface

The language of justification pervades the adjudication of constitutional rights. Rights-claimants must justify their claims about the protections that rights afford, while governments must justify their claims about the restrictions to which rights may be subject. These practices raise a fundamental question: What justifies judgments about constitutional rights? In recent decades, attempts to answer this question have become hopelessly deadlocked.

Among constitutional scholars, the standard view is that constitutional justification raises no distinctive moral principles. Instead, constitutional justification is an exercise in ordinary moral justification. Of course, proponents of the standard view often disagree about what is morally desirable, but they share the broader idea that what morality demands is fully comprehensible and specifiable apart from constitutional law. Constitutional justification, then, is simply moral justification on a larger stage.

My aims in this Element are both critical and constructive. As a critical matter, I will demonstrate that the standard view generates an impasse between two competing theories of constitutional rights. The first engages in legally unconstrained moral reflection to identify the protections that fall within the scope of a right. The second engages in legally unconstrained moral reflection to determine the strength that a right possesses with respect to opposing considerations. While these theories polarize constitutional thought, I will show there is no basis for preferring either one. Each begins by affirming the standard view, and each concludes by (1) abandoning the rule of law, (2) rendering constitutional rights incapable of regulating the exercise of public power, and (3) disregarding constitutional text. In the impasse that ensues, each theory "is able to make the other look quite bad" but unable to defend itself.[1]

As a constructive matter, I will formulate an alternative to the standard view of constitutional justification. I will argue that, far from being an exercise in ordinary moral reasoning, rights-based constitutional order is a distinctive moral project with its own corresponding justificatory method. This method escapes the impasse to which the standard view inevitably succumbs.

---

[1] Ely (1980), p. 111.

The moral project of rights-based constitutionalism consists in rendering all public authority accountable to the inherent rights of each legal subject.[2] Rights-based constitutional order is not synonymous with constitutional rights. Earlier forms of governance recognized that persons are bearers of rights (rather than merely subject to duties); that these rights are inherent (rather than acquired and revocable); that these rights are universal (rather than the preserve of a privileged few); that the basic function of government is to respect and protect these rights (rather than to pursue the private ends of those who happened to hold public power); and that these rights must possess the force of supreme law (rather than ordinary law). However, these innovations failed to confront a basic difficulty. Because legal subjects had no way of vindicating their rights, public authorities remained capable of violating rights with impunity, whether though neglect, inadvertence, or persecution. In short, the presence of constitutional rights did not establish the absence of plenary power.

Rights-based constitutional order confronts this difficulty by introducing a further innovation, the *constitutional complaint*.[3] This practice enables any individual to come before a politically independent judicial body to challenge the validity of any act or omission of any public authority as a violation of a constitutionally guaranteed right. By transforming rights from "a mere guideline of a political, moral, or philosophical nature" into justiciable constitutional norms,[4] rights-based constitutional order reorients the relationship between ruler and ruled. Within rights-based constitutional order, no public authority possesses plenary power and no legal subject stands at the mercy of their government. Instead, rights-based accountability constrains every public authority and safeguards every legal subject.

The emergence of the constitutional complaint raises a new question: What makes the resolution of a constitutional complaint justified? From the standpoint of the standard view, one answers this question by taking the existence of constitutional complaints for granted and then asking, all things considered, how they should be resolved. From this standpoint, there are as many theories of constitutional justification as there are schools of moral philosophy, and any attempt to establish the primacy of a particular theory is fraught with difficulty. However, from the standpoint of the moral project of rights-based constitutional order, the justificatory landscape could not be more different. The practice of constitutional adjudication (and the vast scholarly literature that it has spawned) offers opposing methods of resurrecting plenary power, but only one method

---

[2] Weinrib (2016), ch. 5.   [3] Stourzh (2021), pp. 102–4, 125–9.   [4] Cappelletti (1988), p. 89.

that actualizes the accountability of all public power to rights. I call this method the *system of rights*. My aim in this Element is to articulate its structure and significance.

I proceed as follows. Section 1 explores the impasse of constitutional thought by expounding the standard view, the opposing theories that it generates, and the vulnerabilities that these theories share. Section 2 contrasts this justificatory structure with that of the system of rights. From the standpoint of the standard view, a constitutional judgment is justified only if it corresponds to moral demands that are conceivable and specifiable apart from rights-based constitutional order. In contrast, from the standpoint of the system of rights, a constitutional judgment is justified only if it is supported by a form of reasoning that maintains the accountability of all public power to rights. Unlike the standard view, this form of reasoning can neither be comprehended nor specified apart from rights-based constitutional order.

Sections 3 and 4 elaborate this form of reasoning by exploring two doctrines integral to rights-based constitutional ordering, purposive interpretation and proportionality. Proponents of the standard view typically insist that these doctrines are either dangerous distractions that draw attention away from the freestanding moral considerations that really matter or benign invitations to engage in legally unconstrained moral reflection. In contrast, the system of rights shows that these doctrines play an indispensable role within the distinctive moral project of rights-based constitutional order. From the standpoint of this moral project, what is most striking about these doctrines is that if one abandons even a single component – or if one alters the sequence in which these components appear – the constitutional complaint would fail to render public authority accountable to rights, and legal subjects would find themselves, once again, at the mercy of a plenary power. Accordingly, the structure and substance of these doctrines can be elucidated on constitutional law's own terms. Section 3 justifies purposive interpretation and explains how it regulates judgments concerning the scope of rights, while Section 4 justifies proportionality and explains how it regulates judgments concerning the strength of rights.

Section 5 concludes that the system of rights possesses decisive advantages over the standard view of constitutional justification. The standard view creates an impasse between competing theories that are jointly incapable of taking the rule of law, the regulative character of constitutional rights, or constitutional text seriously. The system of rights, in contrast, avoids each of these difficulties and expounds the normative connection between rights-based constitutional order and its most fundamental doctrines.

1 The Impasse

In his classic essay "Taking Rights Seriously," Ronald Dworkin surveyed the constitutional landscape and observed "two very different models" of constitutional rights.[5] The first defines rights broadly and then balances them against "the demands of society at large."[6] The second regards balancing with suspicion and seeks to carefully delineate the "definition of a particular right."[7]

In the last fifty years, these models have become increasingly systematic and antagonistic. With respect to their systematicity, each model elaborates the structure of constitutional rights and a corresponding method of interpretation and adjudication. With respect to their hostility, each model seeks to establish its superiority by demonstrating that the other defies the rule of law, renders constitutional rights nugatory, and disregards constitutional text.

This section (1) explains why constitutional thought has splintered into these opposing models; (2) formulates a succinct and systematic statement of the structure of each model; (3) shows that each model is vulnerable to the same objections; and (4) traces the vulnerabilities of these models back to their source: the shared idea that constitutional justification is simply ordinary moral justification.

1.1 Bentham's Challenge

More than two centuries ago, when the idea that "[t]he aim of all political association is the preservation of the natural and imprescriptible rights of man"[8] began to transform the practice of constitutional law, the philosopher and social reformer Jeremy Bentham issued a fundamental challenge to all declarations of rights, both "actual and possible."[9] His aim was to show, once and for all, that subjection to plenary power is an ineliminable feature of any legal order. Although the rights formulated in the declarations of his time (and the constitutions of our own) purport to establish a form of legal ordering in which each legal subject is protected from their government, Bentham argued that rights either leave public power unconstrained or supplant it with anarchy.

The structure of Bentham's challenge is simple. Once rights are declared, they must stand in some relationship to legislative authority. Bentham postulated two possible relationships: legislation might exceed the strength of rights

---

[5] Dworkin (1978), p. 197. For discussion, see Bomhoff (2013), p. 188.   [6] *Ibid.*, p. 198.
[7] *Ibid.*, p. 200.   [8] *Declaration of the Rights of Man and of the Citizen* (1789), art. 2.
[9] Bentham's original title was "Pestilential Nonsense Unmasked or A Anatomy of the First Déclaration of Rights (Anno 1791); and of all other Déclarations, actual and possible, of pretended Natural Rights in opposition to legal ones." The essay was later published under the less cumbersome title: "Anarchical Fallacies; Being an Examination of the Declaration of Rights Issued During the French Revolution." On the history of Bentham's essay, see Twining (1975).

or rights might exceed the strength of legislation. Bentham termed the former possibility *legal rights*, the latter *natural rights*.

Legal rights, he explained, coexist with legislative authority but cannot constrain it. If legislation reigns supreme over rights, then a legislative authority may specify the scope of rights by placing their boundaries in whatever location it deems fit. But when the boundaries of rights are established by legislative authority, persons necessarily remain at its mercy: "Suppose a [declaration] to say – no man's liberty shall be abridged, but in such points as it shall be abridged in, by the law. This, we see, is saying nothing: it leaves the law just as free and unfettered as it found it."[10] Rights that are products of legislation afford no protection from legislation.

Whereas legal rights are powerless to constrain legislation, legislation is powerless to constrain natural rights. Because the strength of natural rights exceeds that of legislation, there is no right to which "any government *can*, upon any occasion whatever, abrogate the smallest particle."[11] Natural rights are thus "imprescriptible" (or as we might say, conclusive, peremptory, or inviolable).[12] And because natural rights are formulated in "words and propositions of the most unbounded signification"[13] – for instance, protecting the "[u]nbounded liberty" to do or not do "on every occasion whatever each man pleases"[14] – the scope of natural rights encompasses all conceivable forms of human conduct. Bentham famously denounced this combination of ideas as "nonsense upon stilts"[15] because if rights have both the *strength* of supreme law and a *scope* that extends boundlessly, legislation cannot so much as "stir a step."[16] For Bentham, the very notion that rights reign supreme over legislation imperils legislative authority: "[F]rom this declaration of rights, learn what all other declarations of rights – of rights asserted as against government in general, must ever be, – the rights of anarchy – the order of chaos."[17] In their eagerness to ensure that persons were not placed at the mercy of legislative authority, defenders of natural rights repudiated the very possibility of legislative authority regulating human conduct.

Bentham's challenge asks how rights can be reconciled with legislative authority. If the strength of legislation exceeds that of a right, as in the case of legal

---

[10] Bentham (1843), p. 493. [11] *Ibid.*, pp. 501–2. [12] *Ibid.*, p. 501. [13] *Ibid.*, p. 497.
[14] *Ibid.*, p. 502.
[15] *Ibid.*, p. 502. Without referring to Bentham, Christopher Heath Wellman refers to this combination of ideas as our "pretheoretic conception" of rights. Wellman (1995), p. 281.
[16] Bentham later qualified this point: "All coercive laws, therefore (that is, all laws but constitutional laws, and laws repealing or modifying coercive laws,) and in particular all laws creative of liberty, are, as far as they go, abrogative of liberty. Not here and there a law only – not this or that possible law, but almost all laws, are therefore repugnant to these natural and imprescriptible rights: Consequently null and void, calling for resistance ... " Bentham (1843), p. 503.
[17] *Ibid.*, p. 522.

rights, then the scope of each right lies wherever legislation happens to place it and persons find themselves "at the mercy and good pleasure of the law."[18] Alternately, if the strength of rights exceeds that of legislation, as in the case of natural rights, then rights preclude the very possibility of legislative authority regulating human conduct. Rights, then, are either subordinate to legislative authority or preclusive of its exercise. Between these "two rocks," Bentham maintained, defenders of rights seek a middle ground that does not exist.[19] Whether one affirms legal or natural rights, the simple claim that rights both coexist with legislative authority and yet constrain its exercise has no basis.

Bentham's critique of natural rights is propelled by two ideas: a fundamental insight that every theory of supreme law rights accepts, and a fundamental misconception that every contemporary theory of constitutional rights rejects. The insight is that a theory of constitutional rights must offer an account of both the scope and strength of rights. The *scope* of a right consists in the protections that it secures. The *strength* of a right consists in its power to withstand opposing considerations. Bentham's misconception is that any theory of constitutional rights must claim *both* that rights are boundless in their scope (insofar as they encompass all human conduct) *and* unyielding in their strength (insofar as any legislation that violates a constitutional right is invalid). Bentham's achievement in his famous essay was to show that these claims cannot travel together. What he failed to establish is that these claims exhaust the possible understandings of constitutional rights.

1.2 Two Models of Rights

In the centuries that followed Bentham's intervention, proponents of constitutional rights fragmented into two opposing camps. Each accommodates his insight that if constitutional rights are to regulate (rather than preclude) legislative authority, they cannot be *both* boundless in their scope *and* absolute in their strength. And each camp retains Bentham's understanding of *either* the scope *or* the strength of constitutional rights, while mitigating the rigor of the other component. What I will call the *absolutist* model conceives of rights as unlimited in strength but limited in scope.[20] What I will call the *relativist* model

---

[18] *Ibid.*, p. 510.   [19] *Ibid.*, p. 493.
[20] The absolutist camp includes Justice Hugo Black (of the US Supreme Court), Justice Russell Brown (of the Supreme Court of Canada), Justice Suzanne Côté (of the Supreme Court of Canada), John Finnis, Laurent B. Frantz, Jürgen Habermas, George Letsas, Bradley W. Miller, John Oberdiek, Stavros Tsakyrakis, Francisco J. Urbina, Grégoire Webber, Paul Yowell, and the later works of Ronald Dworkin. The label *absolutism* captures this camp's conception of the strength of rights, while the alternative label *specificationism* captures this camp's narrow conception of scope. While members of this camp converge on the claim that, all-things-considered, moral judgment informs the scope of rights, pervasive disagreements remain with

Table 1 Models of rights

	Benthamite Legal Rights	Benthamite Natural Rights	Absolute Rights	Relative Rights
Scope	Limited	Unlimited	Limited	Unlimited
Strength	Limited	Unlimited	Unlimited	Limited

reverses these commitments by conceiving of rights as limited in strength but unlimited in scope.[21] Each approach mirrors the other's structure: relative rights are broad but subject to restriction; absolute rights are specific but immune from incursion. The structures of Benthamite legal rights, Benthamite natural rights, absolute rights, and relative rights are contrasted in Table 1.

The scope of relative rights encompasses "every form of human activity."[22] They include not only the "classical catalogue" of "freedom of speech, association, religion and privacy, narrowly conceived,"[23] but also "relatively trivial interests."[24] Rights relativism animates the German Federal Constitutional Court's interpretation of Article 2(1) of the *Basic Law* – the right to the free development of one's personality – as a "right to do as one pleases."[25] By conceiving of this right as guaranteeing "freedom of action in a comprehensive sense," the Court has held that persons have a prima facie right to do a variety of "mundane things," including "a right to ride horses through public woods, feed pigeons in public squares, smoke marihuana and bring a particular breed of dogs into the country."[26] Proponents of the relativist model are eager to extend the

---

respect to the nature of morality and the institutional arrangements appropriate to a constitutional regime.

The absolutist theory of constitutional rights parallels the specificationist tradition in moral thought. See, for example, Shafer-Landau (1995) and Wellman (1995).

[21] The relativist camp includes Robert Alexy, Aharon Barak, David Beatty, Moshe Cohen-Eliya, Jamal Greene, Matthias Klatt, Mattias Kumm, Moritz Meister, Kai Möller, Jud Mathews, Iddo Porat, Julian Rivers, Alec Stone Sweet, Lorenzo Zucca, and the early works of Ronald Dworkin. The label *relativism* captures this camp's conception of the strength of rights, while the alternative label *inflationism* captures this camp's broad conception of scope. The absolutist camp is not monolithic. Although its members agree that all-things-considered moral judgment determines the strength of rights, disagreement persists regarding the nature of morality and the roles appropriate for legislative and adjudicative institutions.

Antecedents to the relativist camp include the early modern French Physiocratic tradition and the prima facie moral theory pioneered by Ross (1930), p. 41: "[R]ight acts can be distinguished from wrong acts only as being those which, of all those possible for the agent in the circumstances, have the greatest balance of *prima facie* rightness ... over their *prima facie* wrongness." For elaboration of this tradition in moral philosophy, see, for example, Thomson (1986), Montague (2001), and Frederick (2014).

[22] BVerfGE 80, 137 (1989) [Riding in the Forest]. [23] Kumm (2007), p. 140.
[24] Möller (2012a), p. 3. [25] BVerfGE 80, 137 (1989) [Riding in the Forest].
[26] Kumm (2007), p. 141.

frontiers of constitutional rights still further. Relativist rights protect not only conduct that is moral and amoral, but also conduct that is immoral.[27] If there is a prima facie right to do as one pleases, then there must be a prima facie right to do wrong, whether by engaging in defamation, theft, or even murder.[28]

When the relativist model turns from the scope of rights to their strength, it holds that rights are simply prima facie claims that enjoy "no priority over countervailing considerations of policy."[29] These claims about the scope and strength of rights are connected. Because the scope of a relative right is not confined to matters of *"special importance,"* a relative right possesses no *"special normative force."*[30] Within this model, the central question that constitutional rights raise is not whether a person has a prima facie right to engage in a particular activity. Since Bentham's day, proponents of the relativist model have insisted that persons have a "right to everything indiscriminately."[31] Instead, the central question concerns the strength of rights, more specifically, whether public authorities are justified in restricting a prima facie right in a given context.[32] The relativist answer is that, where the moral reasons that support constitutional protection are outweighed by the reasons that oppose it, a prima facie right is susceptible to restriction. Alternately, where the moral reasons that support constitutional protection outweigh those that oppose it, the restriction of a prima facie right is morally unjustified.[33]

Proponents of the relativist model claim that its virtues extend in two directions. On the one hand, the model purports to capture the appropriate relationship between legislation and morality. Legislative authority is constrained whenever the moral reasons that support constitutional protection outweigh the reasons that oppose it. Conversely, legislative authority is unconstrained whenever the moral reasons that oppose constitutional protection outweigh those that support it. On the other hand, the model claims to illuminate contemporary constitutional practice by offering an integrated explanation of why courts around the world recognize that rights possess a broad scope but a limited strength, as indicated by the presence of limitation clauses and the proliferation of the doctrine of proportionality, which culminates in the balancing of rights against opposing considerations.

---

[27] Möller (2012a), p. 77.
[28] Alexy (2002), pp. 214–5; Barak (2012), p. 42; Möller (2014), p. 165.
[29] Kumm (2007), p. 139; Möller (2014), p. 156.
[30] Möller (2014), p. 166 [italic in the original].
[31] Edelstein (2018), p. 75 (quoting François Quesnay, an eighteenth-century French physiocrat who pioneered the relativist conception of rights).
[32] Kumm (2007), p. 140; Stone Sweet and Mathews (2019), pp. 32–33.
[33] Alexy (2002), p. 336.

The Impasse of Constitutional Rights 9

In the eyes of its absolutist critics, rights relativism represents a "devaluation of [the] moral currency" of rights.[34] Having placed all human conduct within the scope of constitutional rights, the relativist account places "genuine and genuinely inviolable rights, such as the right of an innocent person not to be intentionally or negligently killed ... on the same level as spurious (because inflated) claims of rights," such as the right to kill the innocent.[35] Because the relativist camp insists that constitutional rights protect all human conduct, relativism ultimately dilutes the strength of genuine rights in order to ensure that spurious ones remain susceptible to restriction. In the resulting analysis, both the priority and the purpose of constitutional rights is lost. The priority of constitutional rights is lost because even though relative rights have the status of supreme law, they may be balanced against any consideration that opposes them. The purpose of constitutional rights is lost because relative rights may, in principle, be balanced away. Thus, absolutists complain that the relativist model converts constitutional prohibitions into permissions, with the result that whatever "the Constitution says *cannot* be done *can* be done."[36] Wherever the relativist model prevails, "everything, even those aspects of our life most closely associated with our status as free and equal is, in principle, up for grabs."[37]

Absolutists insist that if we are to retain the simple idea that constitutional rights distinguish permissible from prohibited conduct, then the ideas that animate relativism must be inverted. Constitutional rights must be regarded not as prima facie claims that are forfeited whenever the opposing moral reasons are sufficiently weighty, but as inviolable moral conclusions. This claim about the strength of rights has ramifications for their scope. If a constitutional right prevails over any opposing consideration, the protections that a right affords must be confined to specific claims of overriding moral importance.[38] Whereas conflict is the "natural state" of relative rights,[39] it is an impossibility for absolute rights. When the scope of each right is carefully specified, rights cannot conflict with one another.[40] Nor do conflicts obtain between rights and considerations that are not themselves rights. Absolute rights have priority over such considerations and therefore cannot be opposed by them. So conceived,

---

[34] Finnis (1972), p. 388.   [35] *Ibid.*   [36] Frantz (1962), p. 1445 [italic in the original].
[37] Tsakyrakis (2009), p. 489.
[38] Dworkin (1978), p. 261: "The more limited the range of a principle, the more plausibly it may be said to be absolute."
[39] Greene (2021), p. 114.
[40] On the absoluteness of appropriately specified rights, see Webber (2012), pp. 104, 116, and 124; Dworkin (2006), p. 49. For the unorthodox suggestion that conflicts remain possible even within the absolutist account, see Urbina (2017), p. 249.

absolute rights are "specific high-priority requirements, and thus though their force is great, their scope is narrow."[41]

The central question surrounding the absolutist theory of rights is how one justifies what falls within (and what falls beyond) the adamantine boundary of a right. Absolutism has acquired a reputation for refusing to "disclose whatever reasoning in fact underlies the denial of protection."[42] But sophisticated versions of absolutism delineate the scope of rights in this way:

> [I]t is evident that the assertion, "A has a right to say X to B", has hundreds if not thousands of possible legal meanings. Correspondingly, it has hundreds if not thousands of possible moral meanings within the moral discourse about what the morally just legal system should stipulate concerning acts of communicating X. No one of all these possible meanings is self-evidently the right moral claim. So the only way to specify the meaning of "right" in some claim of right – and then the only way to justify the restriction of the claim to this specified sense of "right" – will be to appeal to some principles which are pertinent in moral discourse but which are not expressed in terms of "rights."[43]

On this view, broadly formulated rights present a multiplicity of possible meanings. Since the scope of a genuine right must be specified, and since the sweeping language in which rights are often formulated does not privilege a single specification, one must determine the scope of a right by reference to "values and principles which need not be expressed in terms of rights."[44] In other words, the scope of a right is to be ascertained by looking to some conception of morality, justice, or practical reason to which the scope of rights must answer and which, on pain of regress, can be fully explicated without reference to constitutional rights. For example, in the case of the right to free expression, one specifies the scope of the right by looking to morality to distinguish between those expressive acts that may be permissibly constrained – for example, perjury, defamation, false advertising, threats of violence, and obscenity – and those that must be permitted without exception – for example,

---

[41] *Ibid.*, p. 221. For a succinct list of absolute rights, see Finnis (1980), p. 225.
[42] Ely (1980), p. 109. See also Klatt and Meister (2012), p. 22; Bomhoff (2013), p. 148.
[43] Finnis (1972), p. 386. For further elaborations of the idea that the scope of rights answer to moral ideas that can be explicated without reference to rights, see Finnis (1980), pp. 214–7; Finnis (2015), pp. 199–200. Here, Finnis explains that his master work, *Natural Law and Natural Rights*, "says nothing about rights until" it elaborates, among other topics, "the first principles of practical thinking and deliberating," "foundational moral principles," "the fundamental types of human association," and "the forms *of justice*." Once these elements are placed on the table, rights arise as their "entailments."
[44] Finnis (1980), p. 198.

"speech that is explicitly political."[45] When the scope of an absolute right is appropriately specified, the right "brooks no restriction."[46]

The absolutist model claims to offer a method that takes both rights and morality seriously. The model takes rights seriously by insisting that they possess decisive strength against legislation. Because absolute rights are not susceptible to balancing, they cannot be balanced away. The model takes morality seriously by empowering it to delineate the scope of rights. When the scope of an absolute right is appropriately specified, rights echo whatever morality demands.

When absolutists attack relativists for indiscriminately placing both genuine and spurious rights in the balance, relativists respond that absolutism does not know itself. On the absolutist view, a genuine right is "designated only after the *final* interaction of *all* of the reasons bearing upon the justifiability of a given action."[47] Once this designation occurs, balancing is precluded because genuine rights are absolute in their strength. However, the absolutist opposition to balancing is more rhetorical than real. Wherever the reasons bearing upon the justifiability of a given action divide into supporting and opposing reasons, absolutism offers no alternative to assessing the weight of the competing reasons. That is what balancing is. Even if absolute rights may not be placed in the balance, the scope of each right is nevertheless "the outcome of an underlying balancing approach."[48] And since the "whole point" of absolutism is to determine the scope of genuine rights without engaging in balancing, the theory relies on the very method it repudiates.[49]

Accordingly, the dispute between rights relativism and absolutism is ultimately about when to apply the label *right*. Whereas relativists apply this label to the *inputs* of balancing, absolutists apply it to the *outputs* of balancing.[50] Once the controversy is framed in this way, relativists maintain that the best approach is the one that balances the reasons that support and oppose constitutional protection in a given context in the most transparent and structured manner. Because absolutists purport to define the scope of rights without engaging in balancing, their inevitable engagements in balancing necessarily lack these qualities.[51]

The leading models of constitutional rights diverge in structure but are similarly morally and institutionally indeterminate.

---

[45] Bork (1971), p. 26. For Bork, this category excludes "scientific, educational, commercial or literary expressions as such" (p. 28). For a more expansive absolutist account, see Meiklejohn (1961), p. 257.
[46] Frantz (1962), p. 1436; Dworkin (2006), p. 49.
[47] Oberdiek (2008), p. 135; Webber (2014), p. 131; Finnis (1985), p. 329.
[48] Rivers (2006), p. 184; Bomhoff (2013), p. 148.   [49] Alexy (2002), p. 209.
[50] Zylberman (2022), p. 554.   [51] Klatt and Meister (2012), p. 21.

The absolutist and relativist models can be coupled with any external moral goal: liberal or communitarian, egalitarian or elitist, deontological or consequentialist, secular or sacred. The difference between these models is not the kinds of external moral goals that rights serve, but whether rights serve these goals with their scope or their strength. Debates between relativists and absolutists remain contentious, but nothing of any moral significance is at stake. When it comes to the question of how public authorities should respond to the various constitutional controversies of the day – whether issues of voting rights and electoral regulation, marriage equality, medical assistance in dying, the rights of prisoners and refugees, access to contraception and abortion, or environmental protection – relativists and absolutists speak in one voice in claiming that the exercise of public authority must conform to some external moral goal. Since each model facilitates the fulfillment of any such goal, their enduring dispute is devoid of any practical significance.

Matters of academic genealogy sometimes obscure the fact that relativism and absolutism can serve the same moral goals. To be sure, leading figures in the relativist camp have been liberals, while prominent absolutists have included social conservatives, scrupulously specifying the scope of constitutional rights to preserve religiously inspired understandings of intimacy, reproduction, and family life.[52] However, the contingency of this alignment is evident from the fact that the same moral goals are equally at home in either model. For example, Robert Alexy and Jürgen Habermas conceive of morality in terms of discourse ethics. However, when it comes to constitutional rights, Alexy leads the relativist paradigm, while Habermas affirms its absolutist counterpart.[53] Whether discourse ethics determines the scope of exceptionless rights or the strength of defeasible ones, discourse ethics inexorably prevails. Because each of the leading models of constitutional rights may be coupled with any external moral goal, opposing models may serve the same external goal.[54]

So too, the same model of rights can house antithetical goals. For example, Ronald Dworkin's liberalism stands in diametric opposition to John Finnis's traditional Catholic worldview. And yet, when it comes to formulating a conception of constitutional rights, each defends the absolutist conviction

---

[52] See, for example, Finnis (1994) and Finnis (2013), pp. 157–1.
[53] Alexy (2002); Habermas (1996), pp. 258–9.
[54] Absolutists sometimes claim that "a conception of rights grounded in a theory of justice can be expected to provide for different duties and obligations than one grounded in a theory of defeasible interests." Webber (2014), p. 132. This is not the case. Whatever conduct falls inside the scope of an absolute right could be recognized by relativists as possessing the strength of a definitive right. And whatever conduct falls outside the scope of an absolute right could be characterized by relativists as possessing merely prima facie strength. On this point, see Alexy (2002), p. 213.

that when the scope of a right is appropriately delineated, it binds without exception.[55]

Just as the leading models of constitutional rights can accommodate any independent moral goal, so too they can accommodate any institutional arrangement. The relativist camp is compatible with judicial abdication to legislative determinations about the strength that rights possess, judicial imperialism that frustrates legislative authority at every turn, and everything in between.[56] The absolutist camp exhibits the same institutional flexibility. Absolutism can be coupled with the idea that the judicial role is to ensure that the exercise of legislative authority conforms to the conclusive constraints that rights impose,[57] or the claim that in a democracy, the appropriate role of the legislature is to delineate the specific boundaries of exceptionless rights.[58] Relativism is as indeterminate about who should have the final say about the strength of rights as absolutism is about who should have the final say about their scope. The dispute between these models lies elsewhere.

The fundamental dispute in constitutional rights theory, then, concerns whether morality at large determines the scope or strength of rights. Having explicated each of the leading models of constitutional rights, I will now argue that whichever side one takes in this dispute, the rule of law retreats, plenary power prevails, and fidelity to constitutional text is abandoned. I take up each of these issues in turn.

1.3 The Rule of Law Retreats

Whether external moral goals regulate the scope or strength of rights, the rule of law and its values of publicity, prospectivity, and consistency are lost.

As we have seen, the relativist model affirms the following ideas: all conduct falls within the scope of some constitutional right; all legislative acts or omissions that impact conduct infringe a constitutional right; acts or omissions that infringe a constitutional right must be justified; justification consists in balancing the reasons that support and oppose constitutional protection in a given context; and, finally, one ascertains the strength of these reasons by engaging in "general practical reasoning" that "lacks the constraining features that otherwise characterise legal reasoning."[59] From the relativist standpoint, the correctness of a judgment concerning the strength of a constitutional right "depends upon value-judgments, which are themselves not controllable by the balancing procedure."[60]

---

[55] Dworkin (2006), p. 49; Finnis (1980), p. 230. For discussion of Dworkin's earlier writings on constitutional rights, which maintain that rights are trumps that may be balanced against other trumps, see Weinrib (2017).
[56] Rivers (2012), pp. 250–1. [57] Rao (2008); Frantz (1962).
[58] Finnis (1985); Webber (2012); and Urbina (2017). [59] Kumm (2018), p. 65.
[60] Alexy (2002), pp. 365–6.

The relativist claim that the strength of a constitutional right is determined by legally unconstrained moral reflection undermines the rule of law. As the absolutist theorist Francisco J. Urbina explains:

> The values associated with [the rule of law] – such as certainty and predictability in human relations – are severely harmed, if not sacrificed, when we make law through legal categories that are so vague that they allow judges to reason morally on what is the best solution to the case, without any effective constraint imposed by the law. The law then becomes uncertain and unpredictable, and there is no guarantee that state power will be bound by clear and previously established legal rules, known by its subject, and applied equally to those in the same situation.[61]

Under rights relativism, what a charter of rights ultimately protects is not a publicly established set of rules and principles articulating a particular understanding of the relationship between free persons and their government. Instead, a charter of rights protects the legally unfettered discretion to use the strength of rights as an instrument for advancing some external moral goal. The constitution is thereby reduced "to a formal shell, which ... admits very different and even heterogenous ideas of order successively and simultaneously, without being upheld by one."[62] There is nothing of the rule of law in this.

However, when absolutists excoriate their relativist counterparts for abandoning the rule of law, they issue an objection that is equally destructive of their own position. As we have seen, the difference between relativism and absolutism is not *whether* legally unconstrained moral reasoning determines what constitutional rights demand, but *how* it does so. Under the relativist regime, one determines the strength of rights by appealing to "first-order political morality."[63] The result is that determinations about the strength of rights (and so too the constitutionality of legislation) are legally unconstrained. If one substitutes the word *strength* for *scope*, the same is true of absolutism. As we have seen, absolutists delineate the scope of rights by engaging in "unencumbered first-order normative argument."[64] The result is that determinations concerning the scope of rights (and so too the constitutionality of legislation) lack legal restraint. Whether one sides with absolutism or relativism, legally unconstrained moral reflection determines what a constitutional right demands. Consequently, constitutional law finds itself incapable of controlling "the flood of variations in the interpretation of the fundamental rights."[65] What a constitutional right requires may shift from judge to judge and from case to case. Accordingly, with respect to any constitutional controversy,

---

[61] Urbina (2017), pp. 147–8. See also Webber (2013). [62] Böckenförde (2016), pp. 286–7.
[63] Kumm (2007), p. 137. [64] Oberdiek (2010), p. 244. [65] Böckenförde (2016), p. 287.

The Impasse of Constitutional Rights 15

legal subjects cannot ascertain what protections their rights afford, and officials cannot determine what duties they owe.

Debates between relativists and absolutists are often staged as though relativists affirm established constitutional practices while absolutists formulate a critical alternative. But neither model can make sense of the two-stage models that structures constitutional adjudication in courts around the world. In the first stage, the rights-claimant bears the burden of establishing the infringement of a constitutional right. In the second, the state bears the burden of justifying any infringement. Relativists and absolutists reject this two-staged model for a common reason: constitutional justification is a matter of legally unconstrained moral reflection, and such reflection occurs in a single stage. Accordingly, relativists and absolutists agree that one of the two stages is superfluous. The question is which one.

Absolutists retain the first stage and jettison the second:

> [O]nly one step is necessary. Courts ask whether a given measure infringes a human right. If so, that measure is in violation of human rights ... In order to establish whether a measure infringes a human right, the court will operate with an understanding of what that human right really requires.[66]

From the absolutist standpoint, the content of a constitutional or human right "will turn on one's understanding of what justice requires."[67] When the scope of a right delineates an exceptionless claim of justice, any limitation contemplated by the second stage must be unjustified insofar as it would permit the very acts and omissions that justice prohibits in the first.

Whereas absolutists embrace the first stage and discard the second, relativists embrace the second and discard the first.[68] From the relativist standpoint, there is no point in delineating "the precise doctrinal boundaries between neighbouring rights, for example, the boundaries between the right to property and freedom of profession, or between freedom of expression and religion."[69] Legislation invariably infringes at least one constitutional right – the liberty to do as one pleases. Thus, the relativist camp locates the fundamental moral question at the second stage, where the moral force of the reasons supporting and opposing protection is considered:

> The focus of constitutional rights adjudication is on the second stage of rights analysis; and hence judges will be inclined not to develop any doctrines ... regarding the first stage if they can resolve the case in a coherent and principled way at the second stage, namely by examining whether there are sufficiently strong reasons for the limitation of the interest at stake.[70]

---

[66] Urbina (2017), p. 247. See also Oberdiek (2010), p. 234; Miller (2008), pp. 94–95.
[67] Webber (2014), p. 128.   [68] Möller (2012a), p. 88.   [69] Ibid.
[70] Möller (2018), p. 142. See also Kumm (2018), p. 65; Cohen-Eliya and Porat (2018), p. 103; Beatty (2004), p. 160.

Table 2 The rule of law

	The Role of Morality	The Retreat of the Rule of Law
The Absolutist Model	Legally unconstrained moral reflection determines the *scope* of constitutional rights.	The idea that legally unconstrained moral reflection determines what a constitutional right requires is incompatible with the rule of law's commitment to publicity, prospectivity, and consistency.
The Relativist Model	Legally unconstrained moral reflection determines the *strength* of constitutional rights.	

From the relativist standpoint, constitutional adjudication concerns the strength of rights as determined by *"moral* argument about the acceptable balance of reasons."[71] Since the consideration of these reasons occurs in the second stage, the first is eliminable.

The rule of law cannot survive the two leading theories of constitutional rights. Absolutists engage in legally unconstrained moral reflection to determine the scope of rights, while relativists engage in legally unconstrained moral reflection to determine their strength. In the case of either theory, judgments concerning the constitutionality of legislation are not constrained by law. For rights-based constitutionalism to coexist with the rule of law, we must reject the idea that legally unconstrained moral reflection determines either the scope or the strength of rights. All-things-considered moral reasoning must find its home in the world of peer review, not judicial review. I summarize the argument in this section in Table 2.

1.4 Plenary Power Returns

In the decades following the moral horrors of the Second World War, peoples around the world reflected on their own particular experiences of "tyranny and oppression by a political power unchecked by machinery both *accessible* to the victims of governmental abuse, and *capable* of restraining such abuse."[72] In the spirit of never again, jurisdictions adopted "a new kind of *constitutional norms, institutions,* and *processes* ... to protect the basic rights of individuals and

---

[71] Möller (2012b), p. 717. See also Kumm (2018), p. 65.
[72] Cappelletti (1985), p. 6 [italic in the original].

groups, including the poor, racial and religious minorities, the young and the old, women and more generally, those traditionally deprived of fair and equal access to the law."[73] By (1) recognizing that *each* legal subject is a bearer of inherent rights, (2) elevating inherent rights to the rank of supreme law, (3) establishing that inherent rights bind all public authorities, and (4) rendering inherent rights justiciable before legally expert and politically independent judicial institutions, rights-based constitutionalism seeks to create a legal order in which no person is simply at the mercy of their government.[74] Rights-based constitutional order is the alternative to forms of governance that subject persons to plenary power.

As we saw in §1.2, not all participants in the debate between absolutists and relativists affirm judicial review. But even among those who do, plenary power is merely relocated from a legislative to an adjudicative body. When absolutism directs the operation of judicial review, judges find themselves legally unconstrained when delineating the scope of rights. Conversely, when relativism directs the operation of judicial review, judges find themselves legally unconstrained when calibrating the strength of rights. In either case, the unconstrained moral reflection of adjudicators is substituted for the unconstrained moral reflection of legislators. While the institutional and argumentative mechanics of plenary power are rearranged, the subjection of legal subjects to plenary power remains intact.

In debates about the structure of constitutional rights, absolutists purport to occupy the "philosophical high ground" by maintaining that rights impose unshakeable moral obligations on public authorities. Every absolute right prevails on every occasion.[75] So long as one's attention remains focussed on considerations of strength, absolute rights appear to protect their bearers. However, this protection proves illusory when one's attention shifts from the strength of absolute rights to their scope. As absolutists explain, the scope of constitutional rights are "conclusions of practical reasoning about what ought to be done,"[76] "simply the entailments of the virtue of justice,"[77] and so on. The difficulty for absolutism, then, is that the claim that rights are indefeasible in strength is meaningless if judges are legally unconstrained when determining the protections that fall within their scope. Whenever the scope of an absolute right is specified, rights-bearers find themselves at the mercy of a plenary power.

---

[73] *Ibid.*, pp. 5, 28 [italic in the original]. Cappelletti refers to these norms, institutions, and processes as *constitutional justice*.
[74] Weinrib (2016), ch. 5.   [75] Kyritsis (2014), p. 396.   [76] Webber (2014), p. 131.
[77] Finnis (2015), p. 200.

Relativism takes the opposite path towards plenary power. Because prima facie rights encompass all human conduct, relativists claim to offer a comprehensive system of rights-protection. All legislative acts and omissions that impact conduct infringe one or more prima facie rights, and thus demand justification. While prima facie rights enjoy no priority over opposing claims, relativists insist that such rights are nevertheless "formidable weapons" that prevail whenever the moral reasons that support constitutional protection outweigh those that oppose it.[78] Relativists are correct to observe that prima facie rights might prevail. But, because relativism maintains that persons have a prima facie right to engage in any conduct whatsoever, the crucial issue is the basis on which judges are to determine the strength that such rights possess in various contexts. Relativism calibrates the strength of rights by directing judges to consider "the correct substantive theory of justice,"[79] "theoretically informed practical reasoning,"[80] and "all the relevant moral considerations."[81] Accordingly, legally unconstrained moral judgment determines whether a prima facie right prevails or must yield to some opposing consideration. Because judges enjoy legally unfettered discretion when they calibrate the strength of rights, judges possess unlimited power over the fate of rights-bearers.

It is no answer for relativists and absolutists to claim that the inability of constitutional rights to constrain moral reflection allows for the most perfect justice. As absolutist critics of relativism have perceptively observed, the reason why legally unconstrained moral reasoning "can achieve the most perfect justice" is that it also "allow[s] for the most perfect injustice."[82] However, absolutists remain serenely unaware of the ramifications of their own objection. If relativism is defective because it is incapable of imposing legal constraints on the moral reflection of judges, then absolutism is defective on the same ground. Within each model, the absence of legal constraint and the absence of legal protection are two sides of the same coin.

The leading models of constitutional rights offer no resistance to the notorious slogan: "Sovereign is he who decides on the exception."[83] Under relativism, the sovereign decides on the exceptions to which rights are subject. Under absolutism, the sovereign decides that what is subject to an exception is not a right. In either case, constitutional rights are incapable of constraining judgments about how public authority should be exercised. Table 3 summarizes the argument in this section.

It is one thing to observe the contemporary world and lament the tendency of regimes to backslide away from arrangements in which constitutional rights

---

[78] Kumm (2007), pp. 139–40.   [79] *Ibid.*, pp. 148–9.
[80] Klatt (2014), p. 899; Alexy (2007), p. 344; Kumm (2007), p. 140.
[81] Möller (2012a), p. 134.   [82] Urbina (2017), pp. 210–1.   [83] Schmitt (2005), p. 5.

Table 3 The return of plenary power

	The Role of Moral Reflection	**The Vulnerability of Rights**
The Absolutist Model	Legally unconstrained moral reflection determines the *scope* of a constitutional right.	Rights may be *defined* away.
The Relativist Model	Legally unconstrained moral reflection determines the *strength* of a constitutional right.	Rights may be *balanced* away.

regulate public authority. It is quite another to insist, with Bentham, that supreme law rights are incapable of regulating public authority. Here, the difference between the leading contemporary models of constitutional rights consists in the particular path that they take towards Bentham's conclusion. This convergence raises a crucial question: Is there a method of justifying claims about the scope and strength of rights that does not betray the moral project of rights-based constitutional order by placing persons at the mercy of their government? I return to this question in Section 2.

1.5 Interpretive Strain

The leading models offer opposing answers to the question of how constitutional rights serve external moral goals. Absolutism claims that rights serve these goals with their scope. Relativism claims that rights serve these goals with their strength. When exposed to the routine provisions of modern charters of rights, each claim generates insuperable interpretive difficulties.

From the standpoint of rights relativism, the scope of the right to liberty (or autonomy) envelops every conceivable form of human conduct. Consequently, the general right to liberty renders a host of other constitutional rights redundant:

> By definition, the scope of the general right to liberty includes the scopes of all specific liberties. From the fact that one is prima facie permitted to do and not to do as one pleases, it follows that one is prima facie permitted to express or not to express one's opinion, to choose or reject a certain career, and so on.[84]

---
[84] Alexy (2002), p. 247.

Once the scope of liberty is enlarged to include all human conduct, less general rights leave no mark on the constitution's meaning. Rights relativism "calls into question the necessity of a set of distinct constitutional rights. Nothing would be lost in theory by simply acknowledging one comprehensive prima facie right to personal autonomy instead."[85] When actual charters of rights situate the right to liberty among other (often painstakingly formulated) rights, they speak in vain.

Whereas relativists are puzzled by the *variety* of constitutional rights, absolutists are puzzled by their *generality*. As we have seen, absolutists insist that the scope of each constitutional right is confined to specific forms of conduct that are "categorically exceptionless."[86] This conviction stands in tension with the sweeping terms in which constitutions often formulate rights, protecting, for example, not the freedom to manifest a particular religious belief or practice on a particular occasion, but freedom of religion; not the right to associate with a particular person to advance a particular project, but freedom of association; and so on. The incongruity between the specificity of absolute rights and the generalities in which constitutional rights are formulated raises a dilemma. If constitutional text is taken seriously, one would expect the scope of a right to have some discernible connection to the language in which it is formulated. Absolutists resist this idea because if rights have a broad scope, the demands issued by one right might conflict with the demands issued by another. And if rights impose conflicting demands, then the absolutist claim that each specified right is exceptionless collapses. Alternately, if absolutists insist that constitutional rights have a narrow scope even when they are formulated in broad and sweeping language, then absolutism is open to the charge that it does not take constitutional text seriously.[87]

Absolutists respond to this dilemma by insisting that any right formulated in general terms is not what it seems: "Rights might be *stated* in general terms ... but rights actually *are* specified, so that the seemingly general right not to be killed, for example, which reads as a right not to be killed *full stop*, is truly the right not to be killed *unjustly*."[88] Thus, the scope of a constitutional right is determined not by reference to the language in which it is formulated or the distinctive role that the particular right plays in the overarching constitutional framework, but by some independent moral theory that specifies exceptions to the general principle that the constitution affirms. As one absolutist puts the point, the "right to life involves an absolute right not to be killed unless I am threatening someone else's life, or unless I commit a capital offense, or

---

[85] Möller (2012a), p. 88. Möller maintains that pragmatic advantages follow from having a plurality of rights. See pp. 89–90.
[86] Finnis (1980), p. 230.   [87] Alexy (2002), p. 212.
[88] Oberdiek (2010), p. 238 [italic in the original]; Webber (2014), p. 134.

The Impasse of Constitutional Rights 21

unless ... "[89] Wherever rights are formulated in broad and sweeping language, absolutists insist that the constitution does not mean what it says.

Just as relativists and absolutists encounter difficulty making sense of the framing of constitutional rights, so too they have difficulty making sense of limitation clauses.

Absolutism maintains that when the scope of a constitutional right is congruent with what is morally justified, the right is not susceptible to restriction. Accordingly, any restriction of any genuine right is morally unjustified. As a matter of constitutional design, absolutists characterize limitation clauses as "unnecessary" because constitutional rights can achieve justice apart from them.[90] When the question arises of how extant limitation clauses should be interpreted, absolutists insist that they must be understood as engaging the scope of rights rather than their strength.[91] On this view, a limitation clause signals that the scope of a constitutional right must be delineated in a morally justifiable manner.

As a general approach to the interpretation of limitation clauses of constitutions and regional and international rights-protecting instruments, the absolutist strategy cannot succeed. The central difficulty is that these clauses often explicitly state that restrictions apply to the scope of rights.[92] The influential limitation clauses that appear in the German *Basic Law,* the *European Convention on Human Rights,* and the *International Covenant on Civil and Political Rights* indicate that the exercise of rights may be subject to justifiable restrictions or interferences.[93] These provisions directly repudiate absolutism's organizing idea that whatever falls within the scope of a right possesses inviolable strength. When confronted by provisions that reject the basic architecture of their model, absolutists insist that these provisions must be disregarded because they employ "uncraftsmanlike language."[94] In this way, absolutism arrogates to itself the power to negate a constitutional norm.

In contrast, the relativist model embraces the idea that the restriction of rights may be justifiable. From the relativist standpoint, morality should have a free hand to balance the reasons that support a right in a given context against those that oppose it, and then restrict the right in part or whole as morality demands.

---

[89] Wellman (1995), p. 277. On the absolutist conception of the right to life, see Oberdiek (2008), p. 128.
[90] Urbina (2017), p. 249.
[91] Finnis (1985), p. 327; Miller (2008), p. 95; Webber (2012), pp. 133–4.
[92] Gardbaum (2014), pp. 280–1.
[93] See for example, Basic Law for the Federal Republic of Germany, Article 2(2); 8(2); 10(2); 11(2); 13(7); 17a(2); 19(1); European Convention on Human Rights, Article 2(3); 8(2); 10(2); 11(2); 18; International Covenant on Civil and Political Rights, Article 12, 19, 21–22.
[94] Finnis (1985), p. 327; Webber (2014), pp. 147–8.

However, relativism has difficulty with actual limitation clauses. For instance, some limitation clauses proscribe any restriction of the core or the essential content of a constitutional right.[95] Consider, for example, article 19(2) of Germany's Basic Law: "In no case may the essence of a basic right be affected."[96] Robert Alexy, the leading theorist of the relativist model, interprets this provision as follows:

> [T]he essential core is what is left over after the balancing test has been carried out. Limitations which correspond to the principle of proportionality do not infringe the essential core, even if they leave nothing left of the constitutional right in an individual case. This reduces the guarantee of an essential core to the principle of proportionality. Since this applies anyways, this would mean that article 19(2) Basic Law simply has declaratory effect.[97]

When confronted by a provision that categorically protects the essence of each right, relativists maintain that the essence of the right is what (if anything) survives balancing in a given context. And since balancing determines the extent to which rights may be restricted in all cases, rights are susceptible to being balanced away in their entirety.[98] Under relativism, a constitutional provision indicating that the core of each right is immune from restriction has no impact on the constitution's meaning.

Instead of offering diverging understandings of how each provision within a charter of rights can be given effect, the leading theories of constitutional rights offer opposing visions of how a charter of rights might give effect to some independent moral goal. When these visions conflict with the text of a charter of rights, both camps distort or discard any provision that is inconsistent with their own theoretical commitments. Whichever model one adopts, the line separating constitutional interpretation from constitutional amendment vanishes, and every constitutional provision is rendered insecure. The argument in this section is summarized in Table 4.

1.6 Conclusion

The idea that constitutional justification is ordinary moral justification has divided constitutional thought into opposing theories that share the same defects. When one applies this justificatory idea to either the scope or strength

---

[95] For discussion, see Brkan (2018); Leijten (2018); Lenaerts (2019).
[96] Basic Law for the Federal Republic of Germany, Article 19(2). On the influence of this article, see Brkan (2018); Lenaerts (2019).
[97] Alexy (2002), p. 192. See also Klatt and Meister (2012), pp. 67–68; Rivers (2006), p. 186.
[98] Alexy (2004), pp. 193, 196. For a parallel passage in the relativist cannon suggesting that, in the German constitutional context, even the "inviolable" ["unantastbar"] right to human dignity may be balanced away, see Klatt and Meister (2012), p. 30.

Table 4 Interpretive strain

	Constitutional Rights	**Limitation Clauses**
Rights Absolutism	The *generality* of rights produces interpretive strain.	The *defeasibility* of rights produces interpretive strain.
Rights Relativism	The *variety* of rights produces interpretive strain.	The *indefeasibility* of rights produces interpretive strain.

of rights, one soon makes three further discoveries. The first is that what constitutional rights require is a matter of legally unconstrained moral judgment. The second is that constitutional rights are powerless to constrain these judgments. The third is that any constitutional provision that impedes the pursuit of an independent moral goal may be distorted or even discarded. The first discovery eviscerates the rule of law, the second resurrects plenary power, and the third denies the authority of constitutional text.

2 Constitutional Justification

In a remarkable article published in 1994, the South African public lawyer Etienne Mureinik expounded the significance of his country's transition from Apartheid to rights-based constitutional order. He famously characterized the new constitution as a bridge that led away from a "culture of authority" towards

> a culture of justification – a culture in which every exercise of power is expected to be justified; in which the leadership given by government rests on the cogency of the case offered in defence of its decisions, not the fear inspired by the force at its command. The new order must be a community built on persuasion, not coercion.[99]

This section explores a single question: What makes a justification cogent?

The two leading theories of constitutional rights, absolutism and relativism, offer the same answer: a justification is cogent when it tracks some moral goal that is fully comprehensible and specifiable apart from constitutional law. From this standpoint, constitutional law has no justificatory resources of its own. Constitutional law remains an empty vessel until it is filled with extrinsic justificatory resources. The previous section explained how this view destroys the rule of law (§1.3), deprives constitutional rights of the power to regulate the exercise of public authority (§1.4), and disregards constitutional text (§1.5).

---

[99] Mureinik (1994), p. 32.

This section formulates an opposing account of constitutional justification. I argue that rights-based constitutionalism possesses its own justificatory standards, which are neither comprehensible nor specifiable apart from rights-based constitutional order. These standards regulate the resolution of constitutional complaints by distinguishing between two forms of reasoning, one which renders public power accountable to rights and another that places legal subjects at the mercy of their government. Within rights-based constitutional order, a justification is cogent if it is supported by the mode of reasoning that maintains the accountability of all public authorities to rights.

2.1 Two Models of Justification

Attempts to justify claims about the scope or strength of constitutional rights presuppose a more basic question: What is justification? There are two ways of answering this question.

The first is Archimedean. While explaining the power of levers, the Greek mathematician Archimedes supposedly claimed that if he had a firm place to stand, he could move the entire world. This metaphor illustrates a long-standing theory in which justification proceeds by (1) observing some seemingly intractable dispute, (2) identifying a "firm and immoveable" point that lies beyond the dispute's boundaries,[100] and (3) appealing to this point to resolve the dispute.[101] By invoking a "starting point" located some distance from the disputed terrain, Archimedeans purport to offer a critical perspective that its inhabitants fail to observe.[102] Justification, on this view, involves standing "outside a whole body of belief" and judging it "as a whole from premises or attitudes that owe nothing to it."[103]

In recent decades, constitutional scholars have increasingly invoked Archimedean justification to resolve enduring debates about what constitutional rights require. When applied to rights-based constitutionalism, Archimedean justification posits a division of labour between morality at large and the constitutional law of a particular jurisdiction. The task of morality at large is to provide a detailed blueprint of what is justified. The task of constitutional law is to give whatever is independently justified the force of supreme law.

The attraction of Archimedean justification lies in its promise to decisively resolve interminable debates about what constitutional rights require. But instead of contracting the domain of disagreement, Archimedean justification extends it in two directions.

---

[100] Descartes (2017), p. 20.   [101] Ripstein (2007), pp. 5–7.   [102] Chapman (2011), p. 182.
[103] Dworkin (1996), p. 88.

First, Archimedean justification generates and perpetuates the dispute between absolutism and relativism. Archimedean justification generates this dispute because its organizing idea – appeal to some external moral referent to determine what constitutional rights demand – is fundamentally ambiguous. As Bentham recognized centuries ago, constitutional rights have two structural features: *scope* (consisting of the protections that the right affords its bearer) and *strength* (consisting of the power of the right to withstand opposing considerations). Because Archimedean justification makes no reference to the structure of a constitutional right, it does not indicate which of these structural features stands in need of justification. There are two ways of responding to this ambiguity. One might stipulate that morality imprints its conclusions by delimiting the scope of constitutional rights. Alternately, one might stipulate that morality imprints its conclusions by calibrating the strength of constitutional rights.[104] The former stipulation culminates in absolutism, while the latter culminates in relativism. The thought here is not that absolutism and relativism happen to affirm Archimedean justification. Rather, Archimedean justification creates absolutism and relativism. These theories are produced by the equivocation that arises when one attempts to apply some freestanding moral theory to the bifurcated structure of a constitutional right.

Once absolutism and relativism emerge, Archimedean justification renders their dispute irresolvable. As we saw in the prior section, there is no basis for privileging either model. Each model is (1) committed to the same conception of justification, (2) equally effective in bringing about any external moral goal, and (3) vulnerable to the same objections.

Archimedean justification invites further disagreement. Once one claims that constitutional rights should bring about some moral goal that can be fully grasped without reference to constitutional law, one must ask: Which independent moral goal should constitutional rights serve? Here Archimedean thought fragments into an array of opposing answers drawn from versions of natural law, the common good, libertarianism, liberalism, conservativism, communitarianism,

---

[104] The originalist idea that historical facts determine the meaning of constitutional norms introduces the same problem. The moment one claims that historical facts determine what constitutional rights demand, one is confronted by a familiar question: Do these facts control the scope or the strength of rights? This question divides originalist thought. On this point, see *Kanter v. Barr*, 919 F.3d 437, 452 (7th Cir. 2019) (Barrett J, dissenting):

> There are competing ways of approaching the constitutionality of gun dispossession laws. Some maintain that there are certain groups of people – for example, violent felons – who fall entirely outside the Second Amendment's scope ... Others maintain that all people have the right to keep and bear arms but that history and tradition support Congress's power to strip certain groups of that right ... [O]ne [approach] uses history and tradition to identify the scope of the right, and the other uses that same body of evidence to identify the scope of the legislature's power to take it away.

perfectionism, feminism, utilitarianism, and so on. The result is that judgments about what constitutional rights demand are dragged in opposing directions by those who share the same conception of justification.

Constitutional scholars often conceive of justification in resolutely Archimedean terms. However, Archimedeanism is simply one conception of justification. Its distinguishing idea is that one understands a thing (constitutional rights) in terms of something else (an independent moral goal). The anti-Archimedean alternative lies in the idea that one understands a thing in terms of what it is rather than what it is not.[105] From the anti-Archimedean standpoint, the justificatory task is not to posit some external moral goal and then treat (either the scope or strength of) constitutional rights as an instrument of its realization, but to identify what is distinctive about rights-based constitutional order and to explore the justificatory ramifications of this distinctiveness.

For those steeped in Archimedean justification, anti-Archimedean justification may seem empty. After all, the call to *Understand thing A in terms of thing A* is hardly illuminating. Accordingly, Archimedeans sometimes claim that their counterparts are caught in a vicious circle, in which any conclusion merely restates the initial premise, establishing nothing.

This objection is perceptive but not decisive. It is perceptive insofar as anti-Archimedean thought moves in a circles. It is not decisive, however, because not all circles are vicious. Complex systems are comprised of multiple parts. Rights-based constitutional order encompasses a variety of components, including a charter formulating supreme law rights that protect each legal subject; provisions setting out the bases for the justified restriction of rights; institutional roles of legislative, executive, and adjudicative actors in the joint project of rights-protection; constitutional doctrines that determine the scope and strength of rights; constitutional conventions; norms governing constitutional amendments; and so on. Instead of stipulating some external moral goal that one or more of these parts should serve or insisting that each part is intelligible in isolation, anti-Archimedean justification conceives of these parts as components of

> an elaborate network, a system, of connected items ... such that the function of each item, each concept, could, from the philosophical point of view, be properly understood only by grasping its connections with the others, its place in the system – perhaps better still, the picture of a set of interlocking systems of such a kind.[106]

---

[105] Chapman (2011), p. 182. See also Rawls (1999), p. 25: "The correct regulative principle of a thing depends on the nature of that thing."
[106] Strawson (1992), p. 19.

Within anti-Archimedean thought, justification operates by identifying the parts of a complex whole, expounding the distinctive contribution that each part makes to the whole, and the way in which the whole captures the commonality of the parts. So conceived, anti-Archimedean thought moves in a circle that elucidates the coherent unity that obtains between the general and particular aspects of a thing.[107] Whether the resulting circle is narrow and empty or wide and illuminating is ultimately "a matter for judgment."[108]

These opposing conceptions of justification draw our attention towards different questions. Archimedean justification asks: What external moral goal should constitutional rights serve? Should the scope or strength of constitutional rights bring about that goal? In contrast, anti-Archimedean thought eschews reference to external moral goals and instead asks: Is there some moral project that is distinctive to rights-based constitutional order? What constraints does this project impose on judgments regarding the scope and strength of rights? Finally, do these constraints avoid the impasse of constitutional rights?

2.2 Rights-Based Constitutional Order

When constitutional lawyers and judges describe the moral significance of rights-based constitutionalism, they often characterize it as "a real revolution," a "phenomenal development," and a "fundamental innovation."[109] Underlying these striking statements, I suggest, is the idea that when one abstracts from the variable features of rights-based constitutional orders scattered around the world – their distinctive histories and cultures, the ways in which they formulate rights and limitations, the doctrines that they employ and the holdings that their courts have handed down – what remains is a moral principle apposite to the relationship between rulers and ruled: every public act or omission is to be accountable to the inherent rights of each legal subject. Stated conversely: no legal subject is to be placed at the mercy of a plenary power. Elsewhere I have explored the roots and ramifications of this principle.[110] Here I can offer only a sketch.

What is a regime of plenary power? And what problem does such a regime raise for the familiar idea that individuals have rights against their government? A regime of plenary power does not necessarily deny that legal subjects have rights against their government. Such a regime might affirm rights held at common law, or pursuant to a statute, or as a matter of widespread political

---

[107] Rawls (1999), p. 19.
[108] Strawson (1992), p. 20. For an illuminating discussion contrasting linear jurisprudence, which proceeds from an extralegal "fixed originating point," and a circular jurisprudence that envelops the law in "a web of strings shaped into a globe or sphere," see Walters (2020), p. 370.
[109] Cappelletti (1985), pp. 6–7; Cappelletti (1986), p. 89.   [110] Weinrib (2016).

consensus. Nor is a regime of plenary power distinguished by the fact that its acts and omissions result in the systematic violation of rights. What distinguishes a regime of plenary power is its *structure*. A regime of plenary power is organized in such a way that (some or all) legal subjects are left without a mode of legal recourse through which their inherent rights can be vindicated. The result is that public authorities can violate those rights with impunity.

A regime of plenary power might be organized in different ways. When public authority rests in the hands of a single person (as in a monarchy or autocracy), every person is subject to plenary power. When public authority rests in the hands of the few (as in an aristocracy or oligarchy), the many are subject to plenary power. Finally, when public authority rests in the hands of the many (as in a majoritarian democracy), the few remain subject to plenary power. In each of these arrangements, whether inherent rights are respected and protected depends upon the very party that rights place under obligation. In the absence of legal structures that enable each legal subject to vindicate her rights, public authorities might ignore a complaint alleging the violation of a right, deny that the complaint amounts to a wrong, or concede the commission of a wrong but withhold a corresponding remedy. Accordingly, public authorities remain capable of violating rights with impunity, whether through neglect, persecution, discrimination, or even the extermination of rights-bearers.

The innovation of rights-based constitutionalism consists in the integration of a set of normative, institutional, and doctrinal commitments that are protective of the inherent rights of every person subject to the rule of law. As a *normative* matter, charters of rights articulate a set of supreme law rights that are to be enjoyed by each legal subject and that bind every public authority. Because these rights are conceived of as legally binding norms rather than mere "political-philosophical declarations," rights-based constitutionalism requires an *institutional* structure for their vindication.[111] This structure enables each legal subject to challenge any public authoritative act or omission that violates any constitutional right by bringing a constitutional complaint to a judicial body that is both accessible to rights-bearers and politically independent. Within rights-based constitutional order, the enjoyment of one's rights does not depend upon the mere good will or forbearance of the very authorities that rights place under obligation. Finally, as a *doctrinal* matter, constitutional practitioners in jurisdictions around the world have developed an anti-Archimedean methodology for resolving disputes about the scope and strength of rights. This methodology, I argue in the ensuing sections, avoids the shared defects of the leading models. Together, these normative, institutional, and doctrinal

---

[111] Cappelletti (1985), p. 6.

commitments create a form of legal order that does not merely acknowledge that each legal subject has rights that bind all public authority but enables each legal subject to hold every public authority accountable to rights-based standards.

The idea that no person should be at the mercy of a plenary power is a normative abstraction. While this idea distinguishes rights-based constitutional practice from other modes of legal organization, it does not provide a fine-grained blueprint of the various rights that persons possess, the ways in which rights may be limited, the remedies that are available when these rights are impermissibly breached, or the forum in which recourse may be sought. The role of positive constitutional law is not to replicate some perfectly determinate vision of morality, but to specify the abstraction that forms the internal moral goal of rights-based constitutional order.

This specification does not entail uniformity. Different normative and institutional arrangements are capable of rendering public authority accountable to the rights of each legal subject. As a normative matter, when it comes to "concretizing" the scope of basic rights, such as free expression, and their interrelationship with other rights, "a variety of national solutions are compatible with the basic guarantee. Universal recognition of freedom of speech does not require uniform legal solutions or interpretation."[112] As an institutional matter, rights-based constitutional order might operate within a legal system that is unitary or federal, unicameral or bicameral, presidential or parliamentary, common law or civil law, and centralized or decentralized in its system of judicial review.

This account of the moral project of rights-based constitutional order cannot be subsumed within an Archimedean justification. As we have seen, Archimedean justification involves the relationship between two elements: an external moral goal and an instrumental means. The moral goal is *external* to rights-based constitutional order insofar as it can be fully comprehended without reference to it. In turn, rights-based constitutional order is conceived of as an *instrumental* means insofar as one might ask whether charters of rights in general, or the scope or strength of rights in particular, are the most effective means of realizing the moral goal. If it turns out that rights-based constitutional order is ineffective in serving the relevant moral goal, it may be discarded in favour of a more potent mechanism. Alternately, if rights-based constitutional order turns out to be an effective instrument, its moral significance consists in its causal power to realize some independent moral goal on an industrial scale.[113]

Rights-based constitutional order is not explicable in terms of the relationship between an external moral goal and an instrumental means. As the long history

---

[112] Grimm (2009), p. 11–22.   [113] Ripstein (2021), p. 25.

of public law illustrates, in the absence of rights that possess the strength of supreme law, that protect each legal subject, that bind each public authority, and that are justiciable before a politically independent judicial body, certain public authorities retain the power to violate the rights of certain subjects with impunity. Instead of forming an instrumental (or possible) means of rendering the rights of each legal subject enforceable against their government, rights-based constitutional order is the *exclusive* means through which this moral project may be realized. To the extent that this form of legal organization is absent, the subjection of persons to plenary power prevails.

Turning from means to ends, the aim of ensuring that no person is subject to plenary power stands in a different relationship to rights-based constitutional order than the external moral goals that animate absolutism and relativism. This aim is *internal* to constitutional law insofar as it has a single domain of application, the constitutional law relationship between rulers and ruled. Beyond this relationship, this aim is "useless and inert."[114] It has nothing to say about the moral assessment of human conduct as such. Accordingly, the alternative to conceiving of rights-based constitutional order as a possible means of achieving some independent moral goal lies in the idea that rights-based constitutional order is uniquely capable of making a distinctively constitutional form of moral practice possible.

2.3 The System of Rights

We can now return to our original question: What does it mean to say that a judgment about a constitutional right is *justified*? Archimedean and anti-Archimedean thought offers different answers to this question.

From the Archimedean standpoint, constitutional justification consists in the conformity of a judgment to some external moral goal – a "brooding omnipresence in the sky."[115] Archimedeanism establishes this conformity through a series of stages. The first locates a fixed moral point that is both fully comprehensible and determinate apart from constitutional law. The second stipulates whether the scope or the strength of rights will serve as the instrument of that goal's fulfillment. The third insists that doctrines that regulate the adjudication of constitutional complaints are either repugnant (insofar as they violate the conclusions that issue from all-things-considered moral reflection) or redundant (insofar as they reproduce the structure of all-things-considered moral reflection). The fourth discards any constitutional provision that stands in the way of any commitment that emerges in the prior stages. In this way,

---

[114] Stone (2011), p. 319.
[115] *Southern Pac. Co. v. Jensen*, 244 US 205, 222 (1917) (Holmes J, dissenting).

The Impasse of Constitutional Rights 31

Archimedean justification explains how judgments about constitutional rights might give effect to fully determinate moral conclusions that obtain independently of them.

In contrast, anti-Archimedean constitutional thought does not begin with fully determinate moral conclusions and then insist that constitutional law is a tool for effectuating them. Instead, the anti-Archimedean approach proceeds through a series of stages that move from abstract towards more concrete ideas about the structure and significance of justification within rights-based constitutional order. The first (and most abstract) idea is that rights-based constitutional order requires a comprehensive form of accountability in which each public authority must answer to the inherent rights of each legal subject. This form of accountability is manifested through the constitutional complaint, the practice that distinguishes rights-based constitutionalism from other forms of governance. The second idea is that constitutional complaints must be adjudicated in accordance with a mode of reasoning that actualizes rights-based accountability rather than modes of reasoning that resurrect or perpetuate plenary power. The third idea is that purposive interpretation and proportionality (as conceptualized in the succeeding sections) formulate the sequence of reasons that actualize rights-based accountability. The fourth idea is that the application of these doctrines to the contours of a particular charter of rights enables the justified resolution of constitutional complaints. Accordingly, from the standpoint of anti-Archimedean justification, constitutional judgment does not replicate some determinate moral conclusion about what is all-things-considered justified. Rather, constitutional judgment must resolve constitutional complaints in accordance with the moral considerations apposite to rights-based constitutional order.

In what follows, my aim is to set out the method of justification apposite to the resolution of constitutional complaints. Because this method focuses on the connection of each constitutional norm to every other rather than constitutional norms taken in isolation, I call this method the *system of rights*. The sections that follow expound the structure of the system of rights by setting out the justificatory constraints that it imposes on judgments that engage the scope and strength of constitutional rights.

In Section 3, I show how the system of rights formulates an alternative to the way in which the leading models conceive of the scope of rights. I argue that the scope of rights neither encompasses all human conduct (as relativism claims) nor is confined to specific conclusions that issue from open-ended moral reasoning (as absolutism maintains). Rather, the scope of each right is worked out through *purposive interpretation*, a doctrine that seeks to understand a charter of rights as a differentiated unity in which each provision draws out some distinctive aspect of the whole and the whole expresses the commonality of each provision. I expound the components that comprise this doctrine, the sequenced structure that obtains among them, and the justificatory constraints that this approach generates. The resulting framework rejects (1) the absolutist idea that one determines the scope of rights by balancing "*all* of the reasons bearing upon the justifiability of a given action,"[116] (2) the relativist idea that all human conduct receives prima facie constitutional protection,[117] and (3) an interpretive conclusion that absolutism and relativism share: interpretive strain is inevitable because one cannot make sense of *both* the generality *and* variety of rights.

Section 4 explores the strength of rights. Setting aside both the absolutist claim that the strength of a right is always decisive, and the relativist claim that the strength of a right is always defeasible, I argue that one cannot identify the strength of a constitutional right in abstraction from the kind of consideration that opposes it. When confronted by considerations that do not sound in a constitutional register – such as majoritarian preference, administrative expediency, non-prohibitive cost, and the imposition of private moral or religious views – each member of the system of rights possesses decisive strength. However, where the constitution does not establish a hierarchy of rights, members of the system of rights do not possess decisive strength against one another. Instead, conflicts between members of the system of rights must be resolved in a manner that respects the equal claim of each right to fulfillment. I argue that this idea imposes a set of limits on (1) the *ends* for which rights may be restricted, (2) the *means* through which rights may be restricted, and (3) the *extent* to which rights may be restricted. These limits on limits determine the strength of rights and form the basis for each of the sequenced stages that comprise the doctrine of proportionality. Finally, I show that the conception of proportionality that operates within the system of rights offers significantly stronger rights-protection than the relativist conception.

Table 5 formulates the way in which the system of rights departs from each of the leading models, conceives of the structure of the scope and strength of rights, and identifies the constitutional doctrines that expound these structures.

Ultimately, the test of these doctrines is not whether they conform to some external moral goal, but whether they escape the impasse of constitutional rights. Accordingly, we must ask: Do these doctrines abandon the rule of law, or do they explain how constitutional law itself constrains judgments concerning the scope and strength of rights? Do these doctrines perpetuate plenary power, or do they contribute to a form of legal ordering in which public authorities are rendered

---

[116] Oberdiek (2008), p. 135; Webber (2014), p. 131; Finnis (1985), p. 329.
[117] Alexy (2002), pp. 214–5; Möller (2012a), p. 77; Möller (2014), p. 165.

Table 5 The system of rights

	Departure	**Structure**	**Doctrine**
Scope	In the absence of an explicit textual directive, the scope of a constitutional right is neither *boundless* (as under the relativist model) nor confined to *highly specific claims* (as under the absolutist model).	The scope of each right reflects its distinctive purpose within the overarching system of rights. In this way, the system of rights seeks to make sense of both the generality and variety of rights.	The doctrine of *purposive interpretation* (as formulated in Section 3) provides a systematic elaboration of this structure.
Strength	In the absence of an explicit textual directive, the strength of a constitutional right is neither *defeasible* (as under the relativist model) nor *indefeasible* (as under the absolutist model).	Constitutional rights possess *indefeasible* strength with respect to sub-constitutional considerations and *defeasible* strength with respect to every equal member of the system of rights. In this way, the system of rights seeks to make sense of the supremacy of rights and their subjection to limitation clauses.	The doctrine of *proportionality* (as formulated in Section 4) provides a systematic elaboration of this structure.

accountable to the inherent rights of each legal subject? Do these doctrines distort and discard familiar constitutional provisions establishing rights and limits, or do they explain how such provisions can operate coherently?

3 The Scope of Rights

The chasm separating the abstract terms in which constitutional rights are formulated and the concrete circumstances to which they apply raises an enduring interpretive challenge: Can judgments about the scope of broadly formulated constitutional rights (guaranteeing freedom of religion, expression, liberty, and so on) be justified and, if so, what form would such a justification take?

Within the world of constitutional theory, responses to this question swing between two extremes, the absolutist claim that genuine rights are confined to specific moral conclusions and the relativist claim that prima facie rights envelop all human conduct. As Alexy observes:

> There are two main constructions of constitutional rights: one is narrow and strict, a second is broad and comprehensive ... These two constructions are nowhere realized in pure form, but they represent different tendencies, and the question of which of them is better is a central question of the interpretation of every constitution that provides for constitutional review.[118]

In what follows, I make no attempt to establish which of these constructions is better. As I argued in Section 1, each construction aspires to the same supposed virtue and occasions the same vices. The virtue consists in transforming a charter of constitutional rights into an instrument for the pursuit of any external moral goal. The vices consist in the disavowal of the rule of law, the subjection of rights-bearers to plenary power, and the disregard of constitutional text. Because theories that possess the same virtue and vices do not stand in a relationship of superior and inferior, my aim in this section is not to elevate one model over the other but to formulate an alternative to both. I will refer to this alternative as *purposive interpretation*.[119]

Purposive interpretation integrates two ideas that the leading models sever. The first idea is affirmed by absolutism but denied by relativism: if constitutional rights are to have priority over other claims, the scope of rights cannot encompass all conceivable claims. The second is affirmed by relativism but denied by absolutism: open-ended moral reflection does not determine the scope of rights. The aim of this section, then, is to explain how purposive interpretation distinguishes between what falls within and what falls beyond the scope of rights without appealing to some external moral referent.

I begin by showing that the relativist and absolutist methods for determining the scope of rights are not exhaustive of possible methods, as constitutional scholars often suppose. I then formulate the components of purposive interpretation, the sequenced structure that obtains among them, and the way in which this sequence constrains judgments about the scope of rights. I conclude by explaining how purposive interpretation avoids the vices of the leading models.

---

[118] Alexy (2003), pp. 131–2.
[119] For a more expansive treatment of purposive interpretation, see Weinrib (2024).

3.1 Beyond Isolationism

Relativism and absolutism offer opposing strategies for determining the scope of constitutional rights. These strategies do not exhaust the possible interpretive methods.

Relativism treats every reason for or against constitutional protection as relevant to a constitutional claim. Prima facie rights represent reasons that support constitutional protection in a given context. These reasons inevitably conflict with others that oppose constitutional protection in that context. Relativism seeks to resolve these conflicts by appealing to some external moral goal to determine (1) the strength of the reasons that support constitutional protection, (2) the strength of the reasons that oppose constitutional protection, and (3) which set of reasons possesses greater strength in the relevant context. Because the integrity of this exercise would be compromised if reasons for constitutional protection were excluded from the analysis, relativism demands "a wide conception of scope."[120] This conception is informed by two inclusive rules:

(1) Everything which has at least one characteristic, which – viewed in isolation – would suffice to bring the matter within the scope of the relevant right, does so, regardless of what other characteristics it has . . .
(2) Within the semantic leeway of the concepts defining the scope, wide interpretations are to be adopted.[121]

The application of these rules to the right to liberty (or autonomy) culminates in a right to do whatever one pleases. Because the right to liberty encompasses all conceivable forms of human conduct, relativism regards the efforts of courts to delineate the scope of rights as a perfunctory exercise culminating in a preordained conclusion: every legislative act or omission that impacts conduct infringes the prima facie right to liberty (and possibly other rights as well). Accordingly, relativism draws attention away from the question of what the scope of a right demands towards the question of what the strength of a right withstands.

Absolutists are critical of the relativist strategy because it elevates *every* claim for and against constitutional protection to the rank of supreme law. This indiscriminate elevation denies constitutional rights any priority over opposing claims. To preserve the priority of rights, absolutists formulate a methodology to determine what falls within and what falls beyond the boundary of a right. Further, absolutists claim that this methodology is the sole alternative to the relativist strategy. To defend the priority of rights one must endorse absolutism.

---

[120] Alexy (2002), p. 210. [121] *Ibid.*

Consider the following constitutional provision: "Everyone has the right to expressive freedom." When confronted by such a capacious provision, absolutists observe that its sweeping terms can be filled with "hundreds if not thousands of possible legal meanings."[122] Since the provision is too amorphous to specify a particular legal meaning, absolutists insist that "the only way" to introduce determinacy is to appeal to some external source of meaning.[123] Finnis captures this idea as follows:

> How is this process of specification and demarcation to be accomplished? ... There is, I think, no alternative but to hold in one's mind's eye some pattern, or range of patterns, of human character, conduct, and interaction in community, and then to choose such specification of rights as tends to favour that pattern, or range of patterns. In other words, one needs some conception of human good, of individual flourishing in a form (or range of forms) of communal life that fosters rather than hinders such flourishing.[124]

Under absolutism, one specifies the scope of a broadly formulated constitutional right by looking to some external moral goal to distinguish between expressive activity that must be categorically protected and expressive activity for which restrictions are permissible or obligatory. Thus, for any expressive act – whether artistic expression, scientific research, public criticism, blasphemy, fighting words, violence, hate speech, sedition, obscenity, and so on – legally unbounded moral reflection determines whether it is constitutionally protected or left to the operation of ordinary law.

Purposive interpretation offers an alternative method for determining the scope of constitutional rights. Purposive interpretation departs from *relativism* by offering resources for distinguishing what falls within and what falls beyond the scope of rights. Purposive interpretation departs from *absolutism* by denying that "the only way" to specify a broadly formulated right involves appealing to an external moral referent.[125] The former departure preserves the priority of rights. The latter explains how the scope of rights can be delimited without engaging in legally unconstrained moral reflection.

Absolutism relies on an assumption that we might term *isolationism*, the idea that interpretation is an effort to grasp the significance of each constitutional provision considered in abstraction from the broader network of constitutional norms in which it is embedded. As we have seen, absolutism (1) focuses on a particular constitutional provision, (2) observes the

---

[122] Finnis (1972), p. 386.   [123] *Ibid*.   [124] Finnis (1980), pp. 319–20.
[125] Finnis (1972), p. 386.

The Impasse of Constitutional Rights

multitude of possible legal meanings that could be attributed to that provision's capacious terms, and, finally, (3) claims that because the broad terms of the provision do not privilege a particular legal meaning, recourse to some independent moral goal is unavoidable. In short, open-ended moral reflection supplies the determinacy that individual constitutional provisions lack.

Constitutional lawyers and judges are often dismissive of the isolationist idea that a charter of rights comprises a series of "watertight compartments"[126] or "insular and discrete" provisions.[127] Isolationism is problematic because it provides no assurance that the meaning assigned to one constitutional provision will not nullify or duplicate the meaning assigned to another, thereby converting an authoritative provision into a dead letter. For example, in the American context absolutists sometimes interpret the First Amendment guarantee of freedom of speech in a manner that denies legal effect to the Equal Protection Clause,[128] while progressives sometimes interpret the Equal Protection Clause in a manner that denies legal effect to the First Amendment.[129] As an interpretive matter, each of these approaches is objectionable for the same reason: constitutional interpretation proceeds from an authoritative legal text and seeks to give effect to the totality of its provisions in the various social realities to which they apply. In contrast, a constitutional amendment creates or revises a legal text by determining which norms shall possess the strength of supreme law. When one constitutional right is interpreted in a manner that denies another effect, the boundary separating constitutional interpretation from constitutional amendment collapses and the authority of every constitutional right is rendered insecure.

Absolutists characterize their model as the sole method for delimiting the scope of rights.[130] This is not the case. The isolationist assumption that one is to ascertain the scope of each constitutional right in abstraction from every other encounters opposition in the integrationist assumption that a "constitution has an inner unity, and the meaning of any one part is linked to that of other provisions."[131] Absolutism is oriented by the isolationist assumption, while purposivism formulates the integrative alternative.

---

[126] *Mills v. The Queen*, [1986] 1 SCR 863 at para 294, 29 DLR (4th) 161 (Wilson J, dissenting).
[127] *R v. Lyons*, [1987] 2 SCR 309 at para 21, 44 DLR (4th) 193 (La Forest J).
[128] Amar (1992), p.152.   [129] Fleming (2004), p. 1465.
[130] Finnis (1980), pp. 319–20; Finnis (1972), p. 386.
[131] I BverfGE 14 (1951) [Southwest Case]. See also *Reference re Secession of Quebec*, [1998] 2 SCR 217 at para 50, 161 DLR (4th) 385.

In what follows, I will sketch the structure of purposive interpretation, explain how this structure departs from both absolutism and relativism, and show how this structure offers a way out of the impasse.

3.2 The Justification of Purposive Interpretation

Constitutions formulate two kinds of norms.[132] The first are *constitutive* of public authority: they create government by allocating and organizing its three kinds of powers – legislative, executive, and judicial. The second are *regulative* of public authority: they affirm standards to which the exercise of public authority must conform.

A constitutional right is a norm that is regulative in kind and relational in structure. A constitutional right is *regulative* insofar as it formulates a standard to which the exercise of public authority must adhere. A constitutional right is *relational* insofar as it abstracts from monadic considerations, whether pertaining to either the fittingness of a public act or the fate of a particular person. Instead, constitutional rights conceive of the entity that possesses the right and the entity that owes the corresponding duty as situated in a unified relationship in which the violation of the duty wrongs the bearer of the right.

Insofar as constitutional rights are regulative of public authority, the interpretation of constitutional rights involves identifying a standard (or what we might call a *purpose*) to which the exercise of public authority must conform and then specifying what that standard requires in some concrete setting. Elaborating on this idea, Grimm explains:

> [T]he *Bundesverfassungsgericht* (Federal Constitutional Court) understands constitutional rights as legal expressions of values, and these values guide the determination of the meaning of a legal norm. They point the interpreter to the purpose of a constitutional norm or the function it is to fulfil. This is already a two-dimensional understanding of a legal norm. However, the purpose ought to be fulfilled in the real world, and this world is constantly changing. *The goal of interpretation is to fulfil the purpose of the norm to the utmost extent under changing conditions.* This means that the segment of social reality in which a constitutional norm shall take effect ... becomes an integral part of interpretation. The consequence is a three-dimensional understanding of constitutional norms: text plus purpose plus context. Analysis of the social reality to which a norm applies is part of the determination of its meaning.[133]

This passage identifies the components of a purposive interpretation: (1) the text of a charter of rights (conceived of as the totality of its semantic meanings), (2) purposes (conceived of as a set of regulative standards that entitle persons

---

[132] Paine (1992), p. 153.   [133] Grimm (2010), p. 44 [italic added for emphasis].

The Impasse of Constitutional Rights 39

to certain public acts and omissions), and (3) context (conceived of as the various social realities in which public authorities are to effectuate the relevant purposes).

Purposive interpretation places these components within a sequenced structure consisting of three ordered stages.[134]

The first concerns the text of a charter of rights. Purposive interpretation maintains that "[t]he language of a constitutional text sets the boundaries of constitutional interpretation."[135] In contrast, non-interpretive doctrines treat constitutional text as merely "presumptively binding and limiting."[136] This presumption allows constitutional text to be rebutted by "changing public values."[137] This allowance is dangerous because it renders a charter of constitutional rights powerless "to withdraw certain subjects from the vicissitudes of political controversy, to place them beyond the reach of majorities and officials, and to establish them as legal principles to be applied by the courts."[138] A constitution that can be disregarded by majorities provides no protection from them.[139] Within purposive interpretation, the authority of constitutional text is conclusive, not presumptive.[140]

The idea that the language in which a constitutional right is formulated establishes the parameters for its interpretation can also be contrasted with the relativist idea that the scope of a constitutional right reflects the broadest semantic meaning that the text can bear. Purposive interpretation rejects this idea too. Where multiple semantic meanings are consistent with the text of a constitutional provision, the broadest one need not be adopted.[141]

---

[134] On structured purposivism, see Feasby (2022). [135] Barak (2005), p. 92.
[136] Brest (1980), p. 237. [137] *Ibid.*, pp. 236, 229.
[138] *West Virginia State Board of Education v. Barnette*, 319 U.S. 624, 638 (1943) (Jackson J).
[139] *S. v. Makwanyane*, 1995 (3) SA 391, para 88 (CC) (Chaskalson P.):

If public opinion were to be decisive there would be no need for constitutional adjudication. The protection of rights could then be left to Parliament, which has a mandate from the public, and is answerable to the public for the way its mandate is exercised, but this would be a return to parliamentary sovereignty, and a retreat from the new legal order established by the 1993 Constitution ... The very reason for establishing the new legal order, and for vesting the power of judicial review of all legislation in the courts, was to protect the rights of minorities and others who cannot protect their rights adequately through the democratic process.

[140] Barak (2005), p. 92.
[141] In a recent case, the Supreme Court of Canada explained that "while *Charter* rights are to be given a purposive interpretation, such interpretation must not overshoot (or, for that matter, undershoot) the actual purpose of the right ... Giving primacy to the text—that is, respecting its established significance as the first factor to consider within the purposive approach – prevents such overshooting." *Quebec (Attorney General) v. 9147–0732 Québec inc.*, 2020 SCC 32 at para 10, [2020] 3 SCR 426 (Brown and Rowe JJ). The relativist model illustrates that giving primacy to the text does not prevent overshooting. As we have seen, relativism assigns rights the broadest possible scope that the provision can bear. The result is that rights encompass all conceivable forms of human conduct – the most extreme form of overshooting imaginable.

The second stage concerns the imputation of a regulative standard to a particular provision. Purposive interpretation conceives of constitutional provisions not as a series of isolated elements, but as members of a system of interlocking standards that work together to regulate the relationship between rulers and ruled. As the Supreme Court of Canada articulates this idea: "Our constitutional Charter must be construed as a system" in which "[e]very component contributes to the meaning as a whole, and the whole gives meaning to its parts."[142] The idea that a charter of rights is an integrated system constrains the standards that may be imputed to a charter of rights. A general standard attributed to a charter of rights is justified to the extent that it captures what is common to each particular provision. Conversely, a standard attributed to a particular provision is adequate to the extent that it "imbues and informs our understanding of the value structure sought to be protected by the Charter as a whole."[143] From the standpoint of purposive interpretation, standards must be justified systematically rather than stipulated piecemeal. The interpretive task, then, is to formulate a coherent system of general and particular standards that together make sense of a constitutional text in whole and part.

This ideal of constitutional coherence imposes a demanding set of interpretive constraints. Because purposive interpretation seeks to identify the distinctive contribution that each provision makes to the whole, the doctrine eschews imputing a purpose to one provision that renders another inert or duplicative: "It cannot be presumed that any clause in the Constitution is intended to be without effect, and therefore such construction is inadmissible unless the words require it."[144] And because purposive interpretation strives to understand how the overarching general purpose (or purposes) of a charter of rights informs each particular provision, the doctrine rejects purposes that are contradictory or mutually indifferent.

The challenge of purposively interpreting a charter of rights resembles that of solving a Rubik's cube. The task is not to move this or that square from one location to another while ignoring how each movement impacts the position of other squares. Rather, the task is to simultaneously situate each square within an overarching pattern. Similarly, the aim of purposive interpretation is not to assign a purpose to a single provision taken in isolation, but to formulate an interlocking set of general and particular purposes that make sense of a constitutional text in whole and part. While the effort to interpret a charter of rights in this way might culminate in rival interpretations, far from posing a threat to the system of rights, this is exactly what it demands: a comprehensive and creative

---

[142] *Dubois v. The Queen*, [1985] 2 SCR 350 at para 43, 23 DLR (4th) 503 (Lamer J).

[143] *R. v. Lyons*, [1987] 2 SCR 309 at para 21, 44 DLR (4th) 193 (La Forest J).

[144] *Marbury v. Madison*, 5 U.S. 1 Cranch 137, 174 (1803) (Marshall CJ).

effort to develop increasingly integrated interpretations. It is striking that so much of what passes for constitutional interpretation is indifferent to this aim.

Some may be skeptical of the idea that every charter of rights should be interpreted in accordance with the ideal of constitutional coherence. Constitutions, one often hears, are created by and for persons whose worldviews and aspirations stand in opposition. These conflicts are resolved by "compromises, truces, tacit forbearances, and mutual accommodations."[145] Accordingly, there is no guarantee that purposive interpretation – or any other interpretive method – will generate constitutional coherence.

This is true, but it is not an objection to purposive interpretation. This doctrine does not claim that every charter of rights is fully coherent. Nor does it claim that the jurisprudence interpreting a charter of rights in a particular time and place is fully coherent. What purposive interpretation claims is that constitutional interpretation is adequate to the extent that it constructs a system of standards that illuminates a charter of rights in whole and part and, in so doing, enables each member of the system of rights to be given effect on the same terms as every other. Of course, it might turn out that a particular charter of rights ultimately defies the doctrine because any attempt to effectuate one provision nullifies another. If this is the case, constitutional interpretation comes to an end because judgments regarding which constitutional provision shall be given effect and which shall be ignored are non-interpretive. In these circumstances, the rule of law demands a constitutional amendment to restore the possibility of interpretation. The critical point is that one cannot determine whether (and the extent to which) an actual charter of rights defies interpretation without engaging in a systematic effort to understand it as a coherent unity of part and whole. This is purposive interpretation's project.

The third and final stage of the purposive sequence explores whether, in a particular context, the public authority has fulfilled the purpose of a particular provision. Where the acts and omissions of public authorities fulfill the right's purpose, the right is secure. Alternately, where the acts and omissions of public authorities fail to fulfill the right's purpose, the right is breached.

Purposive interpretation is a sequential exercise. The second stage presupposes the first because the interpretive task is to specify, not subvert, abstract constitutional language. Accordingly, the interpreter cannot attribute a purpose to the text that its wording cannot bear.[146] The third stage presupposes the second because the interpreter cannot determine whether public acts or omissions in a particular context conform to the relevant provision so long as its internal purpose remains unspecified. Thus, consideration of whether a

---

[145] Smith (1994), p. 189.   [146] Barak (2005), p. 92.

constitutional provision is fulfilled in a given context presupposes a determination of that provision's purpose and the determination of that purpose presupposes fidelity to the semantic meaning of the constitutional text. Figure 1 sketches the sequential structure of purposive interpretation.

While purposive interpretation is not an algorithm, it does constrain the standards that may be attributed to constitutional rights. Consider s. 2(a) of the *Canadian Charter of Rights and Freedoms*: "Everyone has the following fundamental freedoms: (a) freedom of conscience and religion."[147] In determining the meaning of the term 'conscience,' two approaches have been advanced. The first treats conscience and religion as synonymous; whatever standard applies to religion, applies to conscience as well.[148] On this view, s. 2(a) would protect the right of Quakers not to be conscripted into military service, but would deny parallel protection to those whose pacificism rests on secular grounds.

From the standpoint of the system of rights, such an interpretation is objectionable because "'conscience' and 'religion' should not be treated as tautologous if capable of independent, although related, meaning."[149] A more promising line of interpretation would strive to explain the distinctive contributions that freedom of conscience and religion each make to the constitution as a whole and the way in which the whole unifies these distinctive protections. In a seminal Canadian case, Chief Justice Dickson interpreted this provision in accordance with these strictures. With respect to the purposes of the *Charter* as a whole, Dickson explained that it represents a political tradition that affirms the right of dignified persons to make "free and informed decisions."[150] Moving from the general towards the more particular, Dickson explained that freedom of conscience draws out an aspect of this broader freedom by enabling each person to adopt, refine, revise, and act in accordance with their own self-chosen worldviews, so long as they respect the "parallel rights" of others "to hold and manifest beliefs and opinions of their own."[151] Having set out the relationship between the *Charter* as a whole and freedom of conscience, Dickson turned to formulate the relationship between conscience and religion. Freedom of religion, he explains, is "paradigmatic" of freedom

---

[147] Part I of the Constitution Act, 1982, being Schedule B to the Canada Act 1982 (UK), 1982, c 11 [*Charter*].

[148] *Syndicat Northcrest v. Amselem*, 2004 SCC 47 at para 143, [2004] 2 SCR 551 (Bastarache J, dissenting): "Religious precepts constitute a body of objectively identifiable data that permit a distinction to be made between genuine religious beliefs and personal choices or practices that are unrelated to freedom of conscience."

[149] *R v. Morgentaler*, [1988] 1 SCR 30 at 37, 63 OR (2d) 281 (Wilson J, concurring).

[150] *R v. Big M Drug Mart Ltd*, [1985] 1 SCR 295 at para 122, 18 DLR (4th) 321 (Dickson J).

[151] *Ibid.*, at para 123.

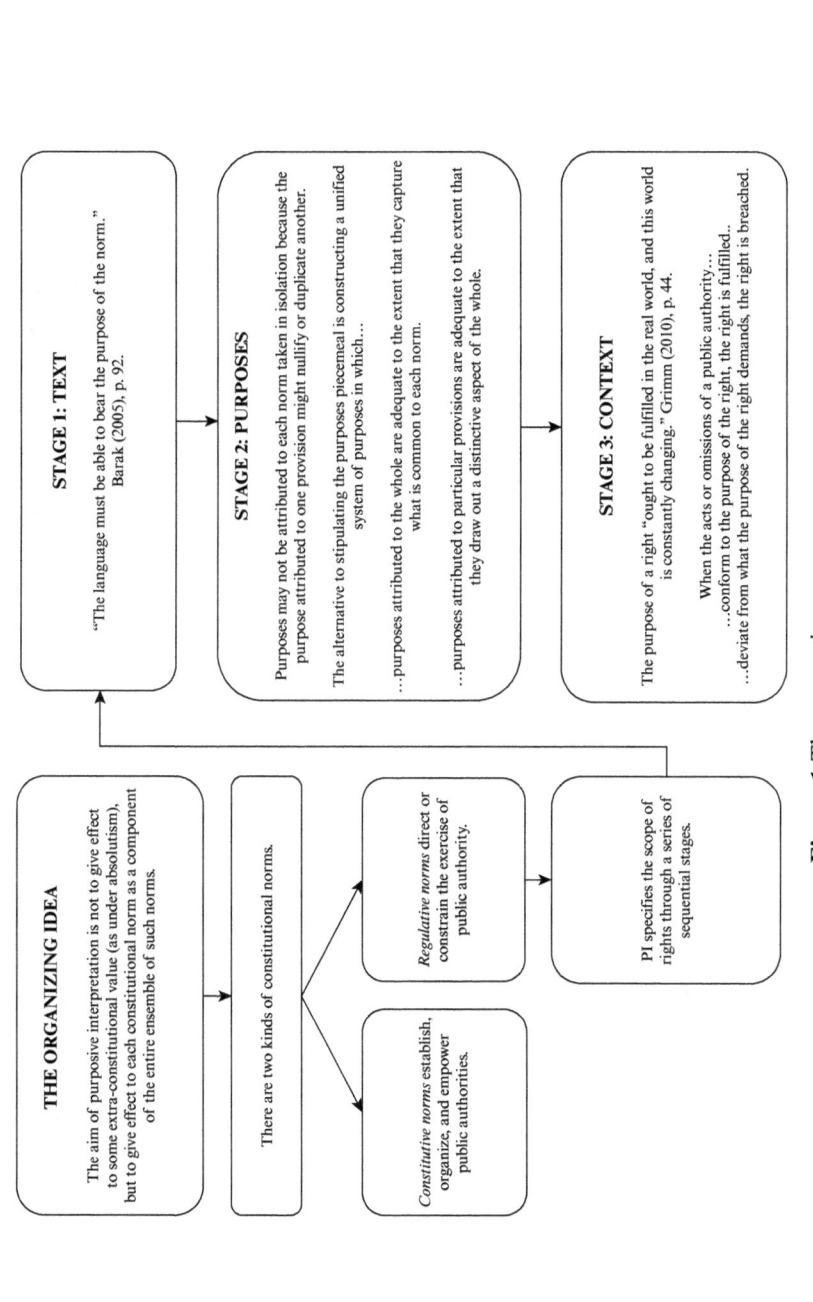

Figure 1 The purposive sequence

of conscience insofar as it prevents government from coercing "individuals to affirm a specific religious belief or to manifest a specific religious practice for a sectarian purpose."[152] On this interpretation, freedom of conscience specifies an aspect of human dignity, and freedom of religion specifies an aspect of freedom of conscience. Accordingly, secular and sacred worldviews are to be afforded equal protection under the *Charter*. Public authorities "cannot incorporate s. 2(a) of the *Charter* in a piecemeal manner" by protecting sacred but not secular worldviews.[153]

There is a long-standing objection to the claim that constitutional protection should extend to non-religious worldviews: "the very concept of ordered liberty precludes allowing every person to make his own standards on matters of conduct in which society as a whole has important interests."[154] Freedom of conscience, on this view, is problematic because it enables any person to raise a constitutional complaint against whatever laws she happens to deem objectionable. The system of rights responds to this objection as follows. Under purposive interpretation, the scope of a constitutional right is determined solely by reference to its own distinctive purpose. This does not mean that other purposes – including the maintenance of the rule of law and the protection of other members of the system of rights – are irrelevant. Rather, their relevance is worked out by reference to a sequence of considerations apposite to the strength of rights. The next section elucidates these considerations.

By conceiving of each constitutional right as a standard situated within a system of rights, purposive interpretation avoids the forms of interpretive strain that absolutism and relativism occasion. As we have seen, absolutism generates interpretive strain by converting a charter of majestic generalities into a series of pin pricks. No matter how broadly constitutional rights are formulated, absolutist rights are confined to highly specific moral claims. In contrast, purposive interpretation affirms the generality of rights by conceiving of them as standards to which public acts and omissions must conform. In turn, relativism generates interpretive strain by insisting that each right is to be afforded its broadest semantic meaning and then observing that liberty renders more specific liberties redundant. In contrast, purposive interpretation proceeds from the presumption that each constitutional provision makes a distinctive contribution to the meaning of the whole. In this way, purposive interpretation accommodates both the generality and variety of rights.

---

[152] *Ibid*.
[153] *Maurice v. Canada (Attorney General)*, (2002) FCT 69 at para 8, 210 DLR (4th) 186 (Campbell J).
[154] *Wisconsin v. Yoder*, 406 U.S. 205, 215 (1972) (Burger, CJ).

Purposive interpretation rejects a further idea to which absolutism is implicitly committed: the scope of a right is the output of a balancing exercise. Section 1 observed that absolutism designates a genuine right "only after the *final* interaction of *all* of the reasons bearing upon the justifiability of a given action."[155] So conceived, absolute rights presuppose balancing but are not subject to it. They presuppose balancing because wherever the reasons concerning the justifiability of a given action stand in opposition, there is no alternative to assessing the relative weight or force of the competing reasons, and that is what balancing is. Absolute rights are not subject to balancing because absolutism affixes the label *right* only to highly specific norms that have survived every possible conflict with every opposing reason.

Unlike absolutism, purposive interpretation determines the scope of rights without engaging in balancing. Balancing is a method of resolving conflicts between competing principles;[156] purposive interpretation does not involve competing principles. Rather, purposive interpretation concerns the relationship between a constitutional text, its purposes, and the various contexts in which public authorities must effectuate those purposes. Text and purpose do not compete. Instead, text constrains the purposes that may be attributed to a provision. Nor do purpose and context compete. Context must conform to purpose. From the standpoint of purposive interpretation, the idea that there is some context to which the purpose of rights must conform is inadmissible because it would render rights powerless to protect persons from various social realities, including historical traditions, societal consensus, and policy preferences. The idea that constitutional standards apply to but are not determined by social reality is built into the sequenced structure of purposive interpretation: when the purpose of a provision is determined, the social reality to which it applies has not yet been considered; when the social reality is considered, the purpose has already been determined. Because determinations about whether (and the extent to which) context conforms to purpose do not involve competing principles, purposive interpretation formulates the scope of rights without balancing.

Purposive interpretation also resists the relativist idea that, absent explicit textual direction, the scope of the constitutional right to liberty encompasses all human conduct. The relativist theorist Kai Möller draws out a striking ramification of this idea: "the murderer, as a moral agent, is entitled to decide for himself whether murdering promotes or ruins the value of his life."[157] Purposive interpretation departs from relativism by delineating the scope of

---

[155] Oberdiek (2008), p. 135; Webber (2014), p. 131; Finnis (1985), p. 329.
[156] Alexy (2002), p. 401.   [157] Möller (2014), p. 165.

a right by reference to its distinctive purpose within the overarching system of rights rather than the broadest semantic meaning that the provision can bear. Whatever the purpose of liberty is within a particular charter of rights, the protections that the right affords must be equally available to everyone to whom the right extends. Murder fails this test because it involves the unilateral extinguishment of another's capacity for liberty. This point affirms an earlier one. Where a charter of rights recognizes that each individual has the right to freedom of conscience, the scope of the right does not extend to conscientious conduct that denies the "parallel rights" of others "to hold and manifest beliefs and opinions of their own."[158] The protections that a right affords cannot contravene its animating purpose.[159]

The system of rights can be further distinguished from absolutism and relativism by considering how each model approaches the possibility and nature of conflicts between constitutional norms.

Under absolutism, when rights are appropriately specified, no conflicts can arise between them. Critics of absolutism have long observed that this position relies on a sleight of hand.[160] Far from avoiding conflicts, absolutists simply refrain from applying the label *right* to any claim unless all possible conflicts with competing norms have been resolved in its favour.

Within the relativist camp, conflicts might be conceptual or contextual. *Conceptual conflicts* arise when the fulfillment of one right necessarily entails the nullification of another, whereas *contextual conflicts* are contingent on particular circumstances. Norms that stand in conceptual conflict always collide; norms that stand in contextual conflict sometimes do. By affirming a right to do as one pleases, relativism generates a multitude of conceptual conflicts: the right to life collides with the right to murder, the right to security of the person collides with the right to torture, the right to equality collides with the right to discriminate, and so on. However, not all conflicts are conceptual. In some circumstances expressive freedom poses no threat to the fulfillment of other members of the system of rights. In other circumstances, expressive freedom conflicts with others' rights to privacy, reputation, or free and fair elections. Absolutism denies the possibility of contextual conflicts because each right occupies its own discrete silo; relativism accepts the possibility of conceptual conflicts because it posits the existence of a right to do as one pleases that is inconsistent with more particular rights.

Purposive interpretation departs from absolutism by accepting the possibility of contextual conflicts and from relativism by precluding conceptual conflicts.

---
[158] *R v. Big M Drug Mart Ltd*, [1985] 1 SCR 295 at para 123, 18 DLR (4th) 321 (Dickson J).
[159] Adams (2018), p. 140.
[160] Alexy (2002), p. 209; Rivers (2006), p. 184; Bomhoff (2013), p. 148.

Contextual conflicts are possible because the scope of each right is determined in light of its own distinctive purpose. It is therefore possible that what falls within the scope of expressive freedom may diminish what falls within the scope of the right to privacy, and vice versa. The next section explores how the system of rights identifies and resolves contextual conflicts. Purposive interpretation does not countenance conceptual conflicts because, absent explicit textual direction, purposive interpretation proceeds on the assumption that each constitutional provision is to be given effect, and provisions that stand in a relation of conceptual conflict cannot be jointly effectuated. The key to giving each constitutional provision effect is to situate each provision within a system of interlocking general and particular standards. Because members of such a system do not stand in relations of conceptual conflict, all conflicts within the system of rights are contextual. The fulfilment of one member of the system of rights does not entail the negation of another.

3.3 Conclusion

Purposive interpretation integrates a series of ideas about the scope of constitutional rights. First, the basic task of a theory of constitutional interpretation is not to stipulate *which* constitutional provisions are to be given effect, but to offer a systematic explanation of how the totality of constitutional provisions can be jointly fulfilled. Accordingly, when imputing purposes to rights, purposive interpretation eschews purposes that render particular provisions contradictory, mutually indifferent, duplicative, or inert and instead seeks to formulate an interlocking set of general and particular purposes that make sense of a charter of rights in whole and part. Second, a charter of rights is a system of standards that regulate the relationship between public authorities and the free persons subject to their governance. Because different constellations of standards may inform different charters of rights, constitutional protections may vary from one jurisdiction to the next. Third, the internal standard of each right must be fulfilled by public authorities in the context of a constantly changing world. So conceived, purposive interpretation identifies the standards that animate a charter of rights and requires public power to live up to them.

Purposive interpretation offers a method of determining the scope of constitutional rights that maintains the rule of law, explains how rights regulate public authority, and avoids the interpretive strain occasioned by opposing models.

Section 1 observed that absolutism creates a crisis for the rule of law by empowering legally unconstrained moral judgment to determine the scope of rights. Purposive interpretation precludes this crisis. The doctrine recognizes the authority of each constitutional right, formulates a network of standards that enable each right to be given effect, and then assesses whether public authorities have acted in conformity with these standards in some concrete setting. In this way, purposive interpretation explains how constitutional law itself constrains judgments regarding the scope of rights.

Further, from the standpoint of purposive interpretation, constitutional rights are standards that regulate the exercise of public authority. The same cannot be said of absolute and relative rights. Under the absolutist model, what regulates public authority is not rights, but the independent moral considerations that determine their scope. The relativist model takes a different route to the same conclusion. Relative rights are incapable of regulating public authority because if every authoritative act or omission breaches a prima facie right, then such rights shed no light on the question of how public authority may be exercised. That question is resolved by providing judges with a legally unconstrained power to determine the strength of rights. In the case of either model, something other than constitutional rights regulates public authority.

Finally, purposive interpretation does not generate interpretive strain by (joining absolutism in) denying the generality of rights or by (joining relativism in) claiming that wherever constitutions entrench a right to liberty, the entrenchment of other rights are in vain. Purposive interpretation recognizes the generality of rights by conceiving of them as standards that regulate the exercise of public authority rather than specific conclusions. Purposive interpretation maintains the variety of rights by presuming that each makes a distinctive contribution to the system in which it stands. From the standpoint of purposive interpretation, a charter of rights is exactly what it purports to be, a set of supreme law standards that supplant the subjection of some or all to plenary power with the protection of each person subject to law's authority.

4 The Strength of Rights

In 1946, mere months after narrowly escaping deportation by the Nazi regime, the German public lawyer Walter Jellinek posed a fundamental question about the relationship between the scope and strength of constitutional rights: "What use is it to say that the first sentence of an article of fundamental rights solemnly guarantees a right, if a second sentence permits restrictions by law?"[161] The leading contemporary theories of constitutional rights offer opposing answers to this question.

From the standpoint of the absolutist model, the scope of a constitutional right is determined by moral reflection. When the scope of a right is morally justified, it follows that any restriction of that right must be morally unjustified.

---

[161] Jellinek (1946), p. 4. See also Poscher (2021).

Accordingly, constitutional rights possess the same peremptory status as the categorical moral claims that they echo. The peremptory strength of rights dictates how absolutists conceive of both limitation clauses and the doctrine of proportionality. Because genuine rights preclude restriction, absolutists stipulate that limitation clauses indicate that it is judgments about the scope (rather than the strength) of rights that must be justified in reference to what morality independently demands. In turn, absolutists brand proportionality – the doctrine that courts around the world employ to determine whether the breach of a constitutional right is justified – as a dangerous confusion that seeks to justify the morally unjustifiable.

Relativism reverses these contentions. With respect to the scope of rights, relativism holds that persons have a prima facie right to engage in whatever conduct that one pleases, whether virtuous, vacuous, or even vicious. The scope of a prima facie right is completely indifferent to moral considerations. But relativists insist that the same cannot be said of the strength of such rights. Prima facie rights may be justifiably restricted whenever the moral reasons that oppose the right possess greater force than the moral reasons that support it. Accordingly, rights possess no priority over the moral reasons that oppose them. Turning from the structure of rights to the purpose of limitation clauses, the relativist model conceives of limitation clauses as the mechanism through which morality asserts itself over the indiscriminate litany of prima facie rights. As for the doctrine of proportionality, relativists conceive of its final balancing substage as providing a structure for the rational assessment of the moral strength of the reasons supporting and opposing constitutional protection in a given context. When unbounded moral reflection determines the strength that prima facie rights possess, morality inevitably prevails.

The prior section focussed on the scope of rights and integrated two ideas that the leading models sever. The first (endorsed by absolutism and denied by relativism) is that, absent explicit textual direction, the scope of rights does not encompass all conceivable forms of human conduct. The second (endorsed by relativism and denied by absolutism) is that the scope of rights is not determined by unconstrained moral reflection. The present section focuses on the strength of rights and, once again, seeks to integrate two ideas that absolutism and relativism separate. The first (endorsed by relativism and denied by absolutism) is that the restriction of a constitutional right may be justified. The second (endorsed by absolutism and denied by relativism) is that the strength of a right is not determined by unconstrained moral reflection. My aim in this section is to explicate the framework in which these commitments coexist.

I proceed in two parts. The first confronts a centuries old skeptical challenge, which alleges that constitutional rights and limitation clauses stand in a relation of conceptual conflict. Constitutional rights, the objection goes, constrain public authorities, while limitation clauses permit whatever rights prohibit. Insofar as rights deny and limitations affirm plenary power, they cannot be jointly given effect. This objection fails. Under a rights-based constitution, the purpose of a limitation clause is not to obliterate rights and thereby resurrect plenary power, but to limit the limits that may be imposed on rights. In the second part, I expound the connection between this purpose and the doctrine of proportionality. Within the system of rights, each stage of the proportionality analysis limits the limits that public authorities may impose on rights. Each of these limits on limits reflects a moral idea distinctive to a regime of constitutional rights: constitutional rights are supreme law standards that possess an equal claim to fulfillment. I explore the doctrinal ramifications of this idea and, in so doing, present a conception of proportionality that departs from the relativist account by preserving the priority of rights and precluding their nullification. I conclude by setting out how this account of the strength of rights escapes the impasse explored in Section 1.

4.1 What's the Point of a Limitation Clause?

Critics and defenders of charters of rights are often puzzled by the fact that these documents typically combine both constitutional rights and limitation clauses that authorize their restriction. The puzzle can be explicated in three steps. The first observes that the purpose of a constitutional right is to constrain legislative authorities. The second claims that the purpose of a limitation clause is to empower legislative authorities to remove whatever constraints rights impose. The third concludes that because rights and limits seek to give effect to antagonistic purposes, they cannot be jointly fulfilled. When a right is taken seriously, it is not subject to a limitation clause; and when a limitation clause is taken seriously, legislative authorities are not burdened by rights. Rights and limits, on this view, stand in a relation of conceptual conflict (§3.2), in which the fulfillment of one nullifies the other. Accordingly, any constitutional text that subjects rights to a limitation clause is fundamentally non-interpretable. After all, interpretation seeks to give effect to the totality of constitutional norms – not to stipulate that certain norms shall be given effect and others ignored.

For centuries, critics and defenders of constitutional rights have appealed to this puzzle to demonstrate that a charter of rights that divides itself between rights and limits cannot stand, and must become all one thing, or all the other. This section presents this puzzle through three of its leading exponents, Jeremy

Bentham, Karl Marx, and Ronald Dworkin. My claim is that the puzzle is generated by the idea that the purpose of a limitation clause is to empower legislative authorities to eviscerate rights. While this idea may resonate with (and indicate the incoherence of) certain constitutional texts, it does not express a general truth about limitation clauses. Where the purpose of a limitation clause is to *limit the limits* to which rights may be subject, constitutional provisions that guarantee rights and that subject rights to limitations may each contribute to a common and coherent constitutional project.

In his excoriating essay on the *Declaration of the Rights of Man and the Citizen*, Bentham insisted that limitation clauses render rights "nugatory."[162] Consider Bentham's gloss on Article 7, which compactly formulates both a right and a limitation: "No one can be accused, arrested or detained but in the cases determined by the law, and according to the forms prescribed by the law."[163] This provision, Bentham thought, cannibalizes itself because the limitation that follows the *but* consumes the right that precedes it. Thus, Bentham held that rights and limitations are contradictory commitments: the point of rights is to constrain legislative power; the point of a limitation clause is to empower legislative bodies to remove the constraints that rights impose. Accordingly, wherever rights are subject to a limitation clause, legislative power remains plenary, and rights-bearers find themselves "at the mercy and good pleasure of the law."[164]

Bentham's claim that rights and limits stand in opposition is rooted in a hierarchical understanding of the relationship between rights and legislation. If rights stand at the normative apex of law's hierarchy, then rights succeed in shackling legislative power. However, where a limitation clause subordinates rights to legislation, rights no longer constrain: "Suppose [a Declaration] to say – no man's liberty shall be abridged, but in such points as it shall be abridged in, by the law. This, we see, is saying nothing: it leaves the law just as free and unfettered as it found it."[165] The reason why rights and limitation clauses

---

[162] Bentham (1843), p. 502. [163] *Declaration of the Rights of Man and the Citizen* (1789).
[164] Bentham (1843), p. 510.
[165] Bentham (1843), p. 493. Perhaps Bentham lost the thread here. As Jellinek explains, the limitation clauses found in the *Declaration of the Rights of Man and the Citizen* "represented an enormous step forward for France in comparison with the legal situation that had prevailed until then, since the administration, i.e. the royal executive, was no longer allowed to act on its own initiative, but only on the basis of legal authorization. From then on, the 'law' empowering the administration had to be a law passed by the people in parliament ... " (Jellinek 1946, p. 4). Far from rendering rights nugatory, as Bentham claimed, these embryonic limitation clauses indicated the limits that rights impose on administrative officials. For a similar argument concerning *prescribed by law* requirements international human rights law, see Garibaldi (1976).

However, if a limitation clause only protects rights from public acts that are not authorized by law, then rights are the beneficiaries of a constraint on public power but not its source. What constrains is the rule of law principle that administrators can act only as authorized by legislation. Accordingly, one could provide an exhaustive account of the constraints on

cannot be jointly effectuated is that rights cannot be both a "barrier against government" and "a barrier which government is expressly called upon to set up where it pleases."[166] Because rights *either* constrain legislative authorities *or* are subject to whatever constraints those authorities might impose, Bentham maintains that declarations of rights exhibit confusion by looking between these "two rocks" for a middle ground that does not exist.[167]

Marx follows Bentham in characterizing the limitation clauses he encountered as constitutional nonsense. In his essay, "The Constitution of the French Republic Adopted November 4, 1848," Marx explains that the fundamental problem raised by the limitation clauses was not that they invite legislative bodies to violate rights, but that they made the violation of rights impossible:

> The reader will at once see that from beginning to end [that the Constitution] is a mass of fine words, hiding a most treacherous design. From its very wording, it is rendered *impossible* to violate it, for every one of its provisions contains its own antithesis – utterly nullifies itself. For instance: – 'the vote is direct and universal', – '*excepting* those cases which the *law* shall determine'. Therefore it cannot be said that the law of May 31, 1850 (disfranchising two-thirds of the people) at all violates the Constitution.[168]

Marx describes the structure of the Constitution of the French Republic as following a two-step pattern. The first formulates sweeping constitutional rights that constrain legislative authorities. The second formulates equally broad limitations empowering those authorities to engage in the very acts and omissions that rights prohibit. The result is that rights provide the illusion of protection, while maintaining the plenary power of legislative institutions. Thus, when the Constitution proclaims "The right of tuition is free. The freedom of tuition shall be enjoyed on the conditions fixed by law," Marx writes that the "old joke is repeated" because the conditions fixed by law "take away the freedom altogether."[169] And when freedom is taken away, one cannot say that the right was *violated* because the limitation permits the very conduct that the right prohibits. Rights that are attended by a limitation clause "carry their own contradiction with them."[170] Because rights that protect nothing cannot be violated, Marx observes that legislation soon converted the French Republic into a "shameless tyranny" without breaching anyone's rights.[171]

Dworkin rejected Bentham's and Marx's skepticism about constitutional rights, but he shared their understanding of limitation clauses. While much of

---

executive authority without referring to constitutional rights. For discussion of this point in the context of German constitutional history, see Grimm (2016), pp. 163–4.

[166] Bentham (1843), p. 515.   [167] Ibid., p. 493.   [168] Marx (2010), p. 577.   [169] Ibid., p. 570
[170] Ibid., p. 578.   [171] Ibid.

Dworkin's immense corpus is devoted to exploring how constitutional rights impose principled constraints on public power, Dworkin said almost nothing about limitation clauses. Even when he observed that "[t]he individual rights that our society acknowledges often conflict,"[172] he refrained from addressing the significance of limitation clauses. Three decades later, in the context of a critical discussion of the detention policies employed by the Bush administration in the war on terror, Dworkin took issue with those who claimed that "no rights can be absolute, there are always circumstances in which government is justified in compromising or ignoring them."[173] Referring to limitation clauses, Dworkin acknowledged that the "great charters of human rights" burden "many of the rights that they list with important qualifications."[174] He then characterized limitation clauses, including those that appear in the *European Convention on Human Rights* as nothing more than "political compromises" formed to elicit the assent of those who are hesitant to subordinate public authority to the discipline of rights.[175] In Dworkin's eyes, limitation clauses are objectionable because they make the principles that animate a charter of rights yield to pragmatic considerations. Accordingly, limitation clauses have no role to play in a regime where principle governs. It is striking that in characterizing limitation clauses as instruments for repudiating rights, Dworkin treated the limitation clauses of contemporary constitutions and international conventions as no different from the ones that Bentham and Marx encountered. This equivalence is mistaken.

In short, for Bentham, Marx, and Dworkin (and contemporary absolutists who invoke their objection), constitutional rights and limitation clauses are not parts of a common project. Rights seek to constrain legislative authorities; limitation clauses invite such authorities to dismantle whatever constraints rights impose. Because limitation clauses permit whatever rights prohibit, each philosopher concludes that charters of rights that couple rights with limitation clauses accomplish nothing.

In philosophic circles, it is commonplace to suppose that the purpose of a limitation clause is to perpetuate plenary power by converting prohibitions concerning public acts and omissions into permissions. However, lawyers – including leading figures in the development of constitutional and international human rights law – frequently claim that limitation clauses have an integral role to play in the project of rights-protection. Their claims raise a fundamental question: Did these lawyers suffer from a confusion that consumed the very rights that they championed, or did they understand something about limitation clauses that generations of philosophers had overlooked?

In an essay entitled "Permissible Limitations on Rights," the influential international lawyer Alexandre Charles Kiss issued a striking statement about

---

[172] Dworkin (1978), p. 193.   [173] Dworkin (2006), p. 48.   [174] *Ibid.*   [175] *Ibid.*, p. 49.

the purpose of the limitation clauses that appear in the *International Covenant on Civil and Political Rights*: "One should always keep in mind that the ultimate objective of the limitation clauses is not to increase the power of a state or government but to ensure the effective enforcement of the rights and freedoms of its inhabitants."[176] This statement extends in two directions. First, it denies that all limitation clauses empower public authorities to "swallow or vitiate" rights.[177] Such a purpose would render the *Covenant* an empty exercise, extending rights with one hand, retracting rights with the other, and ultimately preserving the subjection of persons to plenary power. Second, Kiss's statement suggests that limitation clauses play an essential role in a regime of rights. Kiss's statement is not an aberration. It is commonplace for jurists to refer to limitation clauses as pivotal to the fulfillment of rights.[178] For those who conceive of limitation clauses as perpetuating plenary power, these statements are paradoxical. How could a constitutional provision that authorizes the restriction of constitutional rights contribute to their fulfillment?

Perhaps the clearest answer to this question comes from John P. Humphrey, the international lawyer who authored the influential first draft of the *Universal Declaration of Human Rights*. In a phrase that is as compact as it is significant, Humphrey explained that the purpose of that document's limitation clause "was to put some real limits on limitations of the exercise of freedom."[179] On this view, a limitation clause plays a dual role. On the one hand, a limitation clause "permits the imposition of limitations on the exercise of rights."[180] On the other hand, a limitation clause "puts limits on these limitations."[181] Taking these ideas together, the point of a limitation clause is not to make rights vanish into thin air, but to "protect rights by defining the circumstances and conditions under which they can be limited."[182]

Where a limitation clause limits the limits to which rights may be subject, it is not the case that rights are rendered (1) nugatory (as Bentham claimed), (2) incapable of violation (as Marx maintained), or (3) subordinate to pragmatic considerations (as Dworkin asserted).

Bentham's *two rocks* argument states that rights and legislation that seeks their restriction stand in one of two relations: *either* legislation restricts rights *or*

---

[176] Kiss (1981), p. 310.   [177] *Ibid.*, p. 290.
[178] On the protective function of limitation clauses, see, for example, *Singh v. Minister of Employment and Immigration*, [1985] 1 SCR 177 at para 69, 17 DLR (4th) 422; *Sauvé v. Canada (Chief Electoral Officer)*, 2002 SCC 68 at para 20, [2002] 3 SCR 519; Bielefeldt (2020), p. 19; Grimm (2016), p. 171; Weinrib (2002), pp. 121–2.
[179] Humphrey (1979), p. 147.   [180] *Ibid.*, p. 152.   [181] *Ibid.*
[182] Ahmed and Bulmer (2014), p. 15. Not surprisingly, German constitutional lawyers have a word for the idea that there are limits to the limitations to which rights may be subject: *Shranken-Shranken*. For discussion, see Bielefeldt (2020), p. 14; Grimm (2016), p. 171.

rights restrict legislation. Bentham understood limitation clauses as restricting rights, thereby rendering rights nugatory and legislative authority plenary. But if it were possible to design limitation clauses to impose limits on the limits to which rights may be subject, then a middle ground emerges between Bentham's two rocks consisting of the conditions that distinguish permissible from impermissible limitations. Where a limitation clause establishes such conditions, it is neither the case that legislation always vanquishes rights or that rights always vanquish legislation. When legislation conflicts with rights, whether rights yield to legislation or legislation yields to rights depends upon whether the legislation adheres to the relevant limits on limits. Legislation that deviates from the limits on limits violates supreme law and is therefore unlawful. In contrast, legislation that conforms to the relevant limits on limits lawfully restricts the right. While Bentham directed his *two rocks* objection towards all declarations of rights, he failed to anticipate the possibility of limitation clauses that distinguish between permissible and impermissible limitations of rights. In constitutional jurisdictions around the world, that possibility is now actual.

Similarly, the presence of a limitation clause does not indicate that rights are incapable of violation. When a limitation clause establishes conditions that distinguish between permissible and impermissible constraints on rights, rights continue to constrain wherever those conditions remain unsatisfied. Thus, Marx's claim that limitation clauses leave rights incapable of violation does not express a general truth about limitation clauses. Constitutional rights that are subject to a limitation clause lack absolute strength, but it does not follow that they are incapable of violation.

Finally, if the "main function of limitation clauses is ... to set up criteria by which *to limit the scope of permissible limitations*,"[183] then Dworkin's claim that limitation clauses subordinate principle to pragmatism comes under strain. When a limitation clause limits the limits to which rights may be subject, those restrictions may embody principled considerations. Although Dworkin characterized limitation clauses as unprincipled, his corpus is strewn with passages indicating that when certain limits on limits are respected, rights remain trumps.[184] For example, Dworkin recognized constraints on the *ends* for which rights may be restricted. He insisted that rights may not be limited to advance "ordinary routine goals of political administration," but may be limited to advance "competing rights" and goals of "special urgency."[185] Further, Dworkin imposed constraints on the *means* through which rights may be restricted by insisting that limits actually advance the opposing end[186] and

---

[183] Bielefeldt (2020), p. 4 [italic in the original]. [184] Weinrib (2017).
[185] Dworkin (1978), p. 92. [186] *Ibid.*, pp. 195–6.

that they do so through the least restrictive means.[187] With respect to the *extent* to which a right may be limited, Dworkin maintained that a right cannot be grievously restricted in order to marginally advance the competing right or objective.[188] Indeed, Dworkin even indicated that "government should bear the onus" of justifying limitations on rights.[189] Dworkin's characterization of limitation clauses as intrinsically unprincipled is at variance with his recognition of principles that both restrict rights and respect their status as trumps. As I will explain in Section 4.2, the doctrine of proportionality integrates the various considerations that Dworkin affirms into a sequenced doctrine that enables principled judgments regarding the strength of rights.

If the point of a limitation clause is to eviscerate the constraints that rights impose on government, then rights and limits cannot be jointly given effect. But if some limitation clauses impose limits on the kinds of limits to which rights may be subject, then it is not the case that rights and limits stand in a relation in which the satisfaction of one entails the negation of the other. Limits on limits may be designed and interpreted to preserve the priority of rights over other kinds of considerations and, when claims of right stand in conflict, protect the scope of each right to the greatest possible extent. So conceived, limitation clauses are not "entry points for selling out the substance of human rights," but instead "play a critical role in defending the status and the scope of those rights."[190]

In a rights-protecting constitutional regime, the purpose of a limitation clause is to limit the limits to which rights may be subject, not to preserve plenary power. This claim raises a difficult question: what limits on limits on rights are appropriate?

4.2 The Justification of Proportionality

In courtrooms around the world, judges perceive limitation clauses through the prism of proportionality. The doctrine consists in a set of limits on the limits to which rights may be subject. While these limits on limits shift subtly between constitutional jurisdictions, one prominent version of the doctrine holds that when government seeks to uphold legislation that limits a constitutional right, government must demonstrate that the limitation pursues an appropriate objective; that the limitation employs means that are rationally connected to this objective's fulfillment and minimally impairing of the right; and, finally, that the extent to which the objective is furthered justifies the extent of the right's restriction. When government fails to satisfy any of these conditions, the breach of the right is unjustified.

---

[187] Dworkin (1996), p. 219; Dworkin (1978), p. 204. [188] Dworkin (2006), pp. 24, 26, 50.
[189] Dworkin (1990), p. 11. [190] Bielefeldt (2020), p. 4.

The Impasse of Constitutional Rights

Before we ask whether the doctrine of proportionality can justify the limitation of a constitutional right in a given context, we must confront a more basic question: What is the connection between a limitation clause and the doctrine of proportionality? More specifically, why should a limitation clause be interpreted in terms of the specific limits on limits that the doctrine of proportionality formulates?

While the origins of proportionality are clear, its justification remains murky. Proportionality emerged in the Prussian administrative courts in the late nineteenth century[191] before resurfacing in postwar German constitutional law in the late 1950s.[192] In the decades since, the doctrine has spread to a diverse array of jurisdictions around the globe.[193] Although proportionality is Germany's most significant constitutional export,[194] Germany's Federal Constitutional Court appeals to the doctrine to determine whether limitations of constitutional rights are justified while refraining from offering a justification of the doctrine itself:

> No elaboration of what precisely the source of proportionality is has ever been given. Nor has the Court elaborated how this principle flows from the rule of law or the essence of fundamental rights. The reason for this taciturnity may have been that in Germany ... in the early years the Court was not aware of the prominent role proportionality would play in the future. When this became apparent, the principle had already been established, so that further reasoning seemed unnecessary.[195]

In the absence of a justification, the doctrine of proportionality has been subject to both reductionism and revisionism. *Reductionist* accounts cut down one or more of the doctrine's branches – whether the limits on the ends for which rights may be limited[196] or the limits on the extent to which rights may be limited.[197] *Revisionist* accounts formally retain each of the doctrine's stages, but dilute the analysis, blurring the distinction between permissible and impermissible (1) ends for which rights may be restricted, (2) means through which rights may be restricted, and (3) extents to which rights may be restricted.[198] To the extent that a revisionist account hollows out the limits on limits on rights, plenary power returns.

---

[191] Grimm (2007), pp. 384–5.   [192] BverfGE 7, 377 (1958) [Pharmacy Case].
[193] Barak (2012), p. 182; Cohen-Eliya and Porat (2011); Grimm (2007), p. 384.
[194] Grimm (2010), p. 42.   [195] Grimm (2007), p. 386.
[196] Alexy (2018), p. 19: "[T]he installation of a proper purpose as the first step of proportionality analysis is superfluous ... the Weight Formula allows the impact of the public interests to be set in a relation to all other factors that are relevant for the question of whether the interference with the constitutional right is proportional in the narrower sense."
[197] Hogg (2007), p. 153; Brudner (2009), p. 73; von Bernstorff (2016), p. 71.
[198] See text accompanying notes 241–7.

The relativist model offers the most prominent justification of the doctrine of proportionality. When a limitation clause provides "that an interference with a right is justified if it is, for example, 'necessary in a democratic society,'" relativists claim that the clause "deliberately release[s] judges from interpretative constraints and direct[s] them to the development of a *moral* argument about the acceptable balance of reasons."[199] On this view, limitations clauses are an invitation to engage in open-ended moral reasoning concerning the relative strength of a constitutional right and the considerations that oppose its fulfillment. Proponents of rights relativism affirm competing visions of what all-things-considered morality demands, but they are unified by the idea that proportionality enables conflicts between rights and limits to be resolved in whatever way "the correct substantive theory of justice" requires.[200] To this end, relativists present the doctrine's final substage as a balancing exercise that identifies the moral reasons that support and oppose constitutional protection in a given context, assesses the weight of these reasons, and, finally resolves the conflict in whatever way an external moral goal requires. From the relativist standpoint, the doctrine of proportionality is morally justified because it gives effect to whatever morality at large demands.[201] Call this the *familiar strategy* of justifying proportionality.[202]

In recent years, the familiar strategy has come under heavy fire. On the one hand, critics observe that the familiar strategy imperils the determinacy and predictability to which the rule of law aspires. When the final stage of the proportionality analysis is conceived as an exercise in "general practical reasoning" without the "constraining features that otherwise characterise legal reasoning,"[203] the doctrine resurrects "all the disagreements found within contemporary political philosophy."[204] The result is that wherever the familiar strategy holds sway, whether legislation stands or falls depends on what judges deem morality to demand. On the other hand, critics observe that the familiar strategy renders constitutional law incapable of protecting persons from injustice. Because proportionality is "unrestrained," it "can achieve the most perfect

---

[199] Möller (2012b), p. 717. See also Alexy (2002), pp. 365–6; Klatt (2014), p. 899; and Kumm (2018), p. 65.
[200] Kumm (2007), pp. 148–9; Möller (2014), p. 222; Alexy (2007), p. 344; Klatt (2014), p. 899.
[201] Möller (2012b), pp. 717–8.
[202] The relativist camp is sometimes divided into two approaches, a maximizing approach that conceives of proportionality as a technical structure that seeks to optimise colliding principles and a moralizing approach that conceives of proportionality as inviting unconstrained practical reasoning. Urbina (2017) holds that Alexy exemplifies the former, Kumm and Möller the latter. However, the distinction between these approaches is difficult to maintain because Alexy's maximizing view is itself a hardboiled moralism in which some independent moral goal determines the weight that rights and limits possess. See Alexy (2007), pp. 341–4.
[203] Kumm (2018), p. 65; Kumm (2007), p. 140.   [204] Tremblay (2014), p. 881.

justice. But the same freedom that allows for the most perfect justice can allow for the most perfect injustice."[205] The debate between proportionality's proponents and opponents then shifts to thorny counterfactuals about whether just outcomes would be "more likely in the circumstances of the real world" if proportionality was substituted for some other approach.[206] With this, we find ourselves in the midst of perplexities concerning how the overall balance of just and unjust outcomes attributable to proportionality stack up against the overall balance that would have accrued in the shadow of some other doctrine.[207] Here, constitutional adjudication turns on the hopeless task of comparing the incalculable to the unknowable.[208]

The remainder of this section sketches an alternative to the familiar strategy of justifying proportionality. Instead of conceiving of proportionality as an invitation to calibrate the strength of rights by reference to some freestanding moral goal, I present the stages and sequence of proportionality as a doctrinal distillation of a distinctively constitutional idea: the structure of a system of constitutional rights determines the strength that its members possess.

A system of constitutional rights possesses three structural features that inform this determination. The first is that each member of the system of rights has the status of supreme law. The second is that each member of the system of rights forms a regulative standard to which legislation must conform. The third is that, where the constitution does not establish a hierarchy of rights, each member of the system issues an equal claim to fulfillment. In what follows, I elaborate each of these structural features and explain how they animate the sequenced stages that comprise the doctrine of proportionality. To be sure, my claim is not that the system of rights offers an alternative route to the relativist version of proportionality. Rather, the system of rights alone offers a conception of proportionality that preserves the priority of rights and precludes their nullification.

4.2.1 Limits on Ends: The Appropriate Objective Requirement

Within a regime of plenary legislative power, individual rights enjoy no elevated status. Instead of constraining and directing the exercise of public authority, rights are subordinate to law. Legislative authorities may restrict rights to advance any consideration, whether political or economic, social or cultural. While a regime of plenary power might not balance rights away altogether, it denies rights any priority over other considerations. In contrast, within

---

[205] Urbina (2017), pp. 210–1. [206] *Ibid.*, p. 211; Möller (2014), p. 223.
[207] On the difficulty of assessing constitutional counterfactuals, see Waldron (1999), p. 288.
[208] For a parallel account of counterfactuals in property law theory, see Essert (2024), p. 68.

a rights-based constitutional regime, the laws are subject to individual rights.[209] Each member of the system of rights stands at the normative apex of law's hierarchy and enjoys priority over any legal norm that lacks the same pre-eminence.

The appropriate objective requirement recognizes this priority by imposing a limit on the *ends* for which rights may be restricted: no member of the system of rights may be restricted to advance any legislative objective that does not sound in a constitutional register. Because constitutional rights are supreme law, the pursuit of sub-constitutional objectives might violate rights but cannot justify their limitation. Whenever government seeks to limit a constitutional right, it must justify its position by establishing that the limitation seeks to advance some other norm that possesses constitutional strength, whether another constitutional right,[210] or a constitutional objective that is "essential if man is to continue to enjoy his rights and freedoms."[211] The appropriate objective requirement ensures that when constitutional rights are infringed, the supremacy of every member of the system of rights remains respected.

Absolutist critics of proportionality overlook the appropriate objective requirement when they claim that the doctrine renders everything a matter of weight and degree and that, consequently, "categorical forms of reasoning have no place in proportionality."[212] However, the appropriate objective requirement does not issue the contingent claim that rights typically outweigh sub-constitutional objectives in the balance. Rather, the requirement maintains that because constitutional rights are supreme law, any objective that does not share this elevated status must yield regardless of the benefits that might accrue or the burdens that might be avoided. Accordingly, even if it was possible to substantially further the realization of some sub-constitutional objective by modestly restricting a constitutional right, the restriction would be impermissible. Appealing to the appropriate objective requirement, courts have held that constitutional rights may not be infringed to advance a range of legislative objectives lacking constitutional stature, including majoritarian preference,[213] administrative expediency,[214] non-prohibitive cost,[215] the

---

[209] Dürig (1988), p. 13.
[210] *Gosselin v. Quebec (Attorney General)*, 2002 SCC 84 at para 353, [2002] 4 SCR 429 (Arbour, J, dissenting): "[T]he types of limits that are justified under s. 1 are those, and only those, that not only respect the content of *Charter* rights but also further those rights in some sense – or to use the language of s. 1 itself, 'guarantee' them – by further advancing the values at which they are directed."
[211] Marcic (1968), p. 67.   [212] Urbina (2017), p. 108.
[213] *Sauvé v. Canada (Chief Electoral Officer)*, 2002 SCC 68 at para 20, [2002] 3 SCR 519.
[214] *Singh v. Minister of Employment and Immigration*, [1985] 1 SCR 177 at para 70, 17 DLR (4th) 422.
[215] *Ibid.*, at para 73; *Reference re Remuneration of Judges of the Provincial Court (P.E.I.)*, [1997] 3 SCR 3 at para 284, 150 DLR (4th) 577.

perpetuation of discrimination,[216] and the imposition of private moral or religious views.[217] In each of these instances, rights-based constitutionalism distinguishes itself from a regime of plenary power not by according rights immunity from restriction, but by according rights priority over all sub-constitutional considerations. With respect to such considerations, every constitutional right possesses absolute strength.[218]

The appropriate objective requirement makes a critical departure from the account of proportionality that relativists revere and absolutists abhor.

Relativists determine the strength of prima facie rights by balancing the moral weight of the reasons that support constitutional protection against those that oppose it.[219] Since the strength of a prima facie right is determined through a balancing exercise, it follows that a prima facie right may be balanced against any consideration whatsoever.[220] The fundamental difficulty with this position is not that rights will invariably be balanced away. That is contingent. Rather, the fundamental difficulty is that balancing constitutional rights against considerations that lack the same status deprives constitutional rights of their priority as supreme law norms. Preserving this priority precludes the relativist tendency to "reduce claims of basic liberties or rights of individuals to mere claims of interests" and to "elevate mere claims of interests of government into claims of rights."[221]

Absolutists often criticize proportionality by claiming that the doctrine denies Dworkin's idea that rights are trumps.[222] While relativists typically wash their hands of this idea,[223] the system of rights is committed to it. Recall that the appropriate objective requirement precludes restricting a constitutional

---

[216] *Vriend v. Alberta*, [1998] 1 SCR 493 at para 115, 156 DLR (4th) 385. See also *Bhe and Others v. Khayelitsha Magistrate and Others*, [2004] ZACC 17 at para 72.

[217] *R v. Big M Drug Mart Ltd*, [1985] 1 SCR 295 at para 140, 18 DLR (4th) 321 (Dickson, J); *Minister of Home Affairs and Another v. Fourie and Another*, [2005] ZACC 19 at para 113.

[218] Letsas (2007), p. 117.   [219] Möller (2018), p. 139.

[220] Alexy (2007), pp. 342–4; Möller (2018), p. 139.

[221] Fleming (2004), p. 1446; *cf.* Rivers (2006), p. 180: "By contrast, the conception of proportionality that predominates in continental European contexts is rooted in an assumption that rights and other interests are formally indistinguishable."

[222] Habermas (1996), p. 256; Tsakyrakis (2009), p. 489; Rao (2008), p. 238; Webber (2013), p. 117; Urbina (2017), pp. 108–9.

[223] Beatty (2004), p. 171; Möller (2018), pp. 139–40. Klatt and Meister, however, develop a relativist account that claims fidelity to a version of the rights as trumps view. See Klatt and Meister (2012), p. 23. I cannot provide a full response to this position here, but I will say this. The claim that the rights as trumps view can coexist with rights relativism merits further scrutiny. As a matter of the scope of rights, rights relativism maintains that every interest should be elevated to the rank of a constitutional right. As a matter of the strength of rights, the rights as trumps view maintains that interests are subordinate to rights. These claims are incompatible. Rights and interests cannot *both* occupy a common plane *and* stand in a hierarchical relationship of superior and subordinate.

right to advance the "ordinary routine goals of political administration."[224] Stated conversely, the only basis for restricting one member of the system of rights is to further the realization of another. To put the same point in the language of the rights as trumps model, the doctrine of proportionality identifies and addresses cases in which one trump clashes with another. When the role of the appropriate objective requirement is acknowledged, the supposed incompatibility between proportionality and the idea that rights are trumps dissolves.[225] The result is that whether a right trumps some other trump in a given circumstance is determined by proportionality analysis, but the appropriate objective requirement ensures that no non-trump can ever trump a trump. The same point applies to Habermas's claim that proportionality collapses the "firewall" between constitutional rights and policies, thereby depriving the former of their "strict priority" over the latter.[226] The appropriate objective requirement maintains this firewall by ensuring that every member of the system of rights enjoys unwavering priority over every legal claim that lacks the same pre-eminence.

Aharon Barak observes that there is "no uniform approach in legal literature and case law regarding the requirement that must be met with respect to proper purpose."[227] The leading alternative to the approach that I sketch here is permissive. In putting forth this alternative, Dieter Grimm suggests that its organizing idea is that in a democratic system of government, "[w]hat is important enough to become an object of legislation is a political question and has to be determined *via* the democratic process."[228] On this view, rights may be restricted to advance any objective that the constitution does not explicitly prohibit. While rights may not be balanced against *un*constitutional objectives, they may be balanced against any *sub*-constitutional objective. For example, equality rights may not be restricted to advance a discriminatory objective but may be restricted by (and balanced against) objectives of legislative policy and preference.

By affirming the permissive approach, Grimm generates a tension between his accounts of the scope and strength of rights. In his luminous dissenting opinion in *Riding in the Forest*, Grimm explains that the scope of constitutional rights protect "the integrity, autonomy, and communication of the individual in his basic relations."[229] Because the subject matter of these rights has "fundamental importance" for a legal order "founded on human dignity," they must be "elevated" above other legal claims and "furnished in constitutional law with increased guarantees against public authority and in particular have binding

---

[224] Dworkin (1978), p. 92.   [225] Weinrib (2017).   [226] Habermas (1996), pp. 258, 256.
[227] Barak (2018), p. 330.   [228] Grimm (2007), p. 388.
[229] BVerfGE 80, 137 (1989) [Riding in the Forest].

The Impasse of Constitutional Rights 63

effect on the legislator."[230] However, when Grimm turns from the scope of rights to their strength, he abandons the idea that rights are elevated above ordinary legal claims in favour of the idea that rights may be justifiably restricted to advance sub-constitutional objectives.[231] These accounts of the scope and strength of rights are incongruous: rights cannot be both elevated above considerations of ordinary law and yet remain on par with them.

There are two ways to resolve this incongruity. The first is to adopt the relativist strategy and insist that rights encompass all human conduct and therefore enjoy no priority over considerations of legislative policy and preference. This approach is incompatible with Grimm's claim that what falls within the scope of a constitutional right stands above such considerations. The second is to retain Grimm's approach to the scope of rights and formulate a corresponding account of the strength of rights that acknowledges their supremacy. This Element follows that path.

4.2.2 Limits on Means: Rational Connection and Minimal Impairment

Government cannot justify restricting one member of the system of rights simply by avowing that its objective is to realize another. Even if the appropriate objective requirement is satisfied, it remains possible that the objective is not actually furthered by the means that the law employs. If mere gesturing to some other member of the system swept away the standard that any other member of the system of rights imposes on legislative authority, then it would be possible to play each standard against another, no standard would bind, and legislative authority would remain plenary. Accordingly, proportionality limits not only the *ends* for which rights are restricted, but also the *means* of their restriction. These limits on means take the form of the rational connection and minimal impairment requirements. These requirements reflect the same underlying idea: each member of the system of rights forms a standard to which legislation must give effect.

The rational connection requirement precludes the possibility of limiting one member of the system of rights through means that do not further the realization of another. To satisfy the requirement, government must demonstrate that the means through which a right is restricted are conducive to realizing the law's objective.[232] Because the rational connection requirement is preceded by the appropriate objective requirement, the satisfaction of the rational connection

---

[230] *Ibid.*   [231] Grimm (2007), p. 388.
[232] *R. v. Oakes*, [1986] 1 SCR 103 at para 70; 26 DLR (4th) 200; *Egan v. Canada*, [1995] 2 SCR 513 at para 191, 124 DLR (4th) 609; BVerfGE 55, 159 (1980) [Falconer Hunting License]; *National Coalition for Gay and Lesbian Equality v. Minister of Home Affairs*, 2000 (2) SA 1, at para 56.

requirement establishes that the restriction of one member of the system of rights contributes to the fulfillment of another. In contrast, when the rational connection requirement is breached, justification is impossible. Since each member of the system of rights constrains legislative authority, no member of that system may suffer a gratuitous injury.

The chain of justification extends beyond the rational connection requirement. Even where the rights-infringing means are rationally connected to the appropriate objective, it may be possible to achieve the relevant objective through means that are less injurious of the right. To the extent that this is the case, it is not possible to justify the restriction of one member of the system of rights with reference to the other. Accordingly, to satisfy the minimal impairment requirement, government must demonstrate the absence of an alternative means that would achieve the legislative objective while imposing a lesser injury to the right.[233] When multiple means would be equally effective in realizing the appropriate objective, the legislature must select the least intrusive means. In this way, proportionality analysis denies that legislative authorities possess discretion to diminish one member of the system of rights to a greater extent than the pursuit of another member demands.

The constraints that proportionality imposes on the means through which a right may be limited reflect the idea that each member of the system of rights is a standard to which legislation must conform. The standards that comprise the system of rights are not fulfilled by legislative measures that impede one member of the system without advancing another. Nor are these standards respected by measures that restrict one member to a greater extent than another's claim to fulfillment can justify.

4.2.3 Limits on Extent: The Final Proportionality Substage

When the minimal impairment requirement is satisfied, two (or more) members of the system of rights stand in conflict. If the right is fully realized, the appropriate objective cannot be. And if the objective is fully realized, the right cannot be. The final stage of proportionality addresses the question of how conflicts between members of the system of rights are to be resolved in cases where the constitutional text presents each member "as being of equal validity and rank" and offers "no specific limitations clauses" for addressing conflicts that might obtain between them.[234]

The idea that rights are trumps is powerless to resolve such conflicts. This idea proves decisive only when a constitutional right is confronted by

---

[233] *R. v. Oakes*, [1986] 1 SCR 103 at para 70; 26 DLR (4th) 200; Barak (2012), p. 317.
[234] Marauhn and Ruppel (2008), p. 296.

a sub-constitutional consideration; it offers no resources for resolving conflicts between supreme law norms.[235] Nor may such conflicts be resolved by "postulating an abstract hierarchy" in which one right, say, freedom of expression, always trumps another, say, equality, or vice versa.[236] Where the constitutional text does not situate rights in a hierarchy, invoking any such priority would collapse the boundary separating constitutional interpretation from constitutional amendment. As Justice Iacobucci of the Supreme Court of Canada explained:

> [I]t is not the role of courts to make normative judgments about which rights should be prioritized at the expense of others. However, it is proper for courts to give the fullest possible expression to all relevant Charter rights, having regard to the broader factual context and to the other constitutional values at stake.[237]

The final proportionality substage limits the *extent* of any restriction upon any member of the system of rights. On the one hand, this substage precludes the abject nullification of one member of the system of rights to further the fulfillment of another. On the other hand, the substage precludes substantial interference with one member of the system of rights to modestly further the fulfillment of another.[238] Each of these limits on the permitted extent of limitations upon rights follows from the same underlying idea: members of the system of rights possess an equal claim to fulfillment. Accordingly, where conflicts arise between members of the system of rights, "the question is not to determine which one prevails but to find a solution which leaves the greatest possible effect to both of them (*Pracktische Konkordanz*)."[239] This idea has two aspects, mutual accommodation and contextual application.

First, mutual accommodation distinguishes the final proportionality substage from the minimal impairment requirement that precedes it. Minimal impairment analysis determines whether the conflict between members of the system of rights is overstated, by considering whether there is a means of realizing the relevant objective that is less injurious of the right. Absent a less injurious measure, the minimal impairment requirement would permit any degree of restriction.[240] In contrast, the final proportionality substage does not proceed from the assumption that the objective is "set in stone" and must be achieved "in

---

[235] Zucca (2007), p. xii; Greene (2018), p. 71.
[236] Bielefeldt (2020), pp. 13–14; Fleming (2004), p. 1465.   [237] Iacobucci (2003), p. 140.
[238] HCJ 2056/04 *Beit Sourik Village Council v. Israel*, [2004] IsrSC 58(5) 807; Grimm (2020), p. 115.
[239] Grimm (1994), p. 273.
[240] Barak (2007), p. 373: "Only if it is possible to realize the objects of the statute by less drastic means does this step grant protection to human rights."

its complete integrity."²⁴¹ Because each member of the system of rights has an equal claim to fulfillment, members stand in a relation of reciprocal determination in which each member may restrict and in turn be restricted by every other.²⁴²

Next, contextual application determines whether a member of the system of rights restricts or is restricted by another member. Where members of the system of rights issue an equal claim to fulfillment, conflicts between them cannot be resolved in abstraction:

> The contextual approach attempts to bring into sharp relief the aspect of the right or freedom which is truly at stake in the case as well as the relevant aspects of any values in competition with it. It seems to be more sensitive to the reality of the dilemma posed by the particular facts and therefore more conducive to finding a fair and just compromise between the two competing values ...²⁴³

In different contexts, members of the system of rights might be restricted and fulfilled to varying degrees. The more a legislative act (or an administrative decision) frustrates the purpose of the right, the more severely the right is infringed. For example, the purpose (or purposes) underlying freedom of expression may be impacted more severely by a restriction on political expression than by a restriction on the publication of intimate details of a matrimonial dispute.²⁴⁴ Conversely, the extent to which the restriction of a right furthers some competing member of the system of rights is similarly variable. The final proportionality substage protects the equal claim of each member of the system of rights to fulfillment by permitting mutual adjustments in which members of the system of rights may be restricted at their periphery so that "as much as possible of the original protective content of each is preserved."²⁴⁵ Where the final proportionality substage is satisfied, the purpose of a particular right is breached, but the underlying purposes of the system of rights are maximally realized. In this way, proportionality ensures that the specific members of the system of rights "can operate together as parts of [a] single, coherent account of legitimate state action."²⁴⁶

In our collective constitutional terminology and imagination, the metaphor of balancing has become intertwined with the final proportionality substage. Relativism seeks to develop a rigorous formula that captures the metaphor's

---

²⁴¹ *Alberta v. Hutterian Brethren of Wilson Colony*, 2009 SCC 37 at paras 201 and 195, [2009] 2 SCR 567 (LeBel, J, dissenting).
²⁴² Schladebach (2014), p. 271.
²⁴³ *Edmonton Journal v. Alberta (Attorney General)*, [1989] 2 SCR 1326 at 1355-1356, 64 DLR (4th) 577 (Wilson J, concurring).
²⁴⁴ *Ibid.*, p. 1355.   ²⁴⁵ Schladebach (2014), p. 271.   ²⁴⁶ Thorburn (2016), p. 306.

essence.[247] The system of rights warns that the metaphor invites two dangerous distortions.

First, according to the relativist model, the final substage is a balancing exercise in which one weighs the moral reasons that support and oppose constitutional protection in a given context.[248] Since the strength of a right is determined by balancing it against whatever considerations oppose it, a right may be balanced against any consideration.

The system of rights opposes this conclusion. As we have seen, the final proportionality substage is preceded by the appropriate objective requirement, which maintains that each right, by virtue of its status as a supreme law norm, enjoys priority over any legal norm that lacks constitutional stature. Accordingly, the final proportionality substage applies to the relationship between members of the system of rights, not to the relations between members of that system and sub-constitutional considerations. Considerations of legislative policy, administrative convenience, and private moral or religious views might violate rights, but cannot justify their limitation.

Second, the relativist model permits the restriction of any right to any extent – even a right's complete negation – when the gains to be achieved (or the burdens to be avoided) possess sufficient weight.[249] From the standpoint of the system of rights, the abject sacrifice of any member of the system of rights is not *typically unjustified* but *necessarily unjustifiable*. For the negation of a member of the system of rights can neither be justified by appealing to a sub-constitutional consideration nor to another member of the system of rights. In the former case, justification is precluded by the priority of each member of the system of rights over any sub-constitutional legal norm. In the latter, justification is precluded because if each member of the system of rights issues an equally valid claim to fulfillment, no member can justify another's negation. Accordingly, there is no consideration capable of justifying the negation of a constitutional right. *Limitations* might be justified or unjustified; *negations* are unjustifiable as such.[250] Even where a constitutional right is subject to a limitation clause, government does not possess plenary power with respect to the right's purpose.

To summarize: the doctrine of proportionality consists in a set of limits on the limits to which rights may be subject: limits on the *ends* for which rights may be limited (the appropriate objective requirement), limits on the *means* through which rights may be limited (the rational connection and minimal impairment requirements), and limits on the *extent* to which rights may be limited (the final proportionality substage). Each of these limits on limits is rooted in a structural feature of

---

[247] Alexy (2021). [248] Alexy (2002), p. 210.
[249] Ibid., p. 193; Klatt and Meister (2012), pp. 31–32, 67–68; Rivers (2006), pp. 186–7.
[250] For elaboration of the ideas here, see Örücü (1986); Lenaerts (2019); Weinrib (forthcoming).

Table 6 The strength of rights

Within a system of constitutional rights	The system of rights limits ...	Limitations on rights must ...
... each right is supreme law.	... the *ends* for which rights may be limited.	... pursue an appropriate (constitutional) objective.
... legislation must conform to each right.	... the *means* through which rights may be limited.	... employ means that are rationally connected to the objective and that achieve the objective in a manner that is minimally impairing of the right.
... that establishes no hierarchy among its members, each member has an equal claim to fulfillment.	... the *extent* to which rights may be limited.	... ensure that the extent of the objective's achievement justifies the extent of the right's restriction.

the system of rights. The limit on ends reflects the rank of constitutional rights as supreme law norms. The limits on means reflect the character of rights as supreme law standards to which legislation must conform. The limit on the extent of a restriction reflects the equal claim of each member of the system of rights to fulfillment. In sum, the limitation of a particular right is justified when it respects the organizing structure of the system of rights. These ideas are collected in Table 6.

The structure of the system of rights provides a standpoint for distinguishing proportionality from revisionist accounts of the doctrine, which parrot proportionality's distinctive terminology while diluting or dissolving the limits on limits that proportionality encompasses. First, revisionist accounts dismantle the limits on the *ends* for which a right may be restricted. Instead of asking whether the objective furthers a member of the system of rights, revisionist accounts inquire into the "statutory objective"[251] or the "communal values" the legislation seeks to advance.[252] In the resulting analysis, constitutional rights may be limited by any objective that legislation pursues, and the priority of constitutional rights possess is lost. Second, revisionist accounts dilute the

---

[251] *Doré v. Barreau du Québec*, 2012 SCC 12, [2012] 1 SCR 395 at para 55 (Abella J).
[252] *Sauvé v. Canada (Chief Electoral Officer)*, 2002 SCC 68 at para 82, [2002] 3 SCR 519 (Gonthier J, dissenting).

limits on the *means* through which rights may be restricted. Instead of asking whether the means that the law employs are rationally connected to an appropriate objective, the doctrine asks whether government had a "reasonable basis" for believing that the law was rationally connected to the statutory objective.[253] And instead of insisting that the law pursues an appropriate objective through means that are minimally impairing of the right, revisionist accounts emphasize that the "impugned measures need not be the least impairing option"[254] or the "least intrusive solution."[255] Accordingly, revisionist accounts do not conceive of rights as standards to which legislation must conform. Third, revisionist accounts give rise to a balancing of costs and benefits that recognizes no limits on the *extent* to which a right may be restricted.[256] The result is that the entire scope of a right is susceptible to being balanced away if that would, however trivially, further the realization of the legislative objective. When each of the limits on limits are dissolved, plenary power reasserts itself because any right may be restricted for the sake of any objective, through any means, and to any extent. From the standpoint of a regime that seeks to protect rights-bearers from plenary power, the central question concerning the strength of rights is not whether proportionality will be applied. It is whether the requirements that comprise the doctrine limit the limits to which rights are subject or limit the power of rights to protect their bearers. The former possibility preserves the protective character of rights; the latter perpetuates plenary power and thereby betrays the organizing idea of rights-based constitutional order.

4.3 Conclusion

The system of rights offers an alternative to the way in which absolutism and relativism justify judgments about the strength of constitutional rights.

From the absolutist standpoint, rights might be violated, but their restriction can never be justified. If every constitutional right echoes an exceptionless moral requirement, any restriction of any right is morally unjustifiable. Thus, absolutists collapse the distinction between justified limitations and unjustified violations of rights: to limit (infringe, breach, restrict, etc.) a right is to violate it.[257]

---

[253] *RJR-MacDonald v. Canada*, [1995] 3 SCR 199 at para. 82, 127 DLR (4th) 1 (La Forest J, dissenting).
[254] *Harper v. Canada*, 2004 SCC 33 at para 110, [2004] 1 SCR 827 (Bastarache J).
[255] *Multani v. Commission Scolaire Marguerite Bourgeoys*, 2006 SCC 6 at para 50, [2006] 1 SCR 256 (Charron J).
[256] See, for example, *Quebec (Attorney General) v. A*, 2013 SCC 5 at para 450, [2013] 1 SCR 61.
[257] Webber (2012), p. 124: "Rights, once properly specified, can never be justifiably infringed; they are either complied with or violated – there is no in-between."

The system of rights defends this distinction. From the standpoint of the system of rights, justified limitations and violations are similar in one respect and dissimilar in another. They are similar in that each breaches the scope of a particular right, leaving the relevant standard unfulfilled in a given context. They are dissimilar in that each stands in a different relationship to the system of rights. *Limitations* are justified when they respect each of the organizing ideas of the system of rights – the idea that members of this system are supreme law, that legislation must conform to each member of the system, and that (in the absence of a constitutional text establishing a hierarchy of rights) each member of the system of rights possesses an equal claim to fulfillment. In contrast, *violations* breach not only a particular right but also one or more of the organizing ideas of the system in which rights stand.[258] From the standpoint of these ideas, limitation and violation are not equivalent terms.

From the relativist standpoint, the strength that a right or a limit possesses in a given context is a "question of substantive moral and political theory."[259] Because determinations about the strength of rights depend upon "premises provided from the outside,"[260] proportionality "inherit[s] all the unreliability and all the imponderabilia of those substantial, political, moral, and contested propositions which are used as normative premises in applying the law of balancing."[261] The system of rights takes a different path. Instead of relying on an external moral goal to determine the strength of rights, the system of rights determines the strength of its members in light of a set of distinctively constitutional moral commitments acknowledging (1) that constitutional rights are supreme law standards that bind public authorities, (2) that public authorities must conform to these standards, and (3) that conflicts between equal members of the system of rights must be resolved in a manner that preserves as much as possible of each. External moral goals play no role in this analysis.

In determining the strength of rights, the system of rights does not abandon the rule of law, resurrect plenary power, or generate interpretive strain.

The system of rights does not abandon the rule of law because it does not follow the relativists in treating limitation clauses as an invitation to engage in legally unconstrained moral reflection to determine whether a right or a limitation should prevail in a given context. Instead, the restriction of a particular right is justified when it respects the organizing ideas of a system of rights and unjustified to the extent that it effaces them.

---

[258] L. Weinrib (2002), p. 121: "A limitation attests to the primacy of that which it limits and maintains some conceptual continuity with it, coming into play only upon demonstration of stringent justifying conditions. In contrast, abrogation nullifies that which it abrogates. It is the traditional role of courts to sustain this distinction wherever it arises in our legal system."
[259] Alexy (2007), p. 341.   [260] *Ibid.*, p. 344.   [261] Klatt (2014), p. 899.

Further, the system of rights does not resurrect plenary power. Because the "power of the public authority to impose limitations is itself limited,"[262] rights continue to constrain public authority. Together, the limits on limits operate to uphold constitutional rights as members of a set of supreme law standards that public authorities must increasingly fulfill.

Finally, the system of rights avoids the interpretative strain that the absolutist and relativist conception of the strength of rights generates. As we saw in Section 1, the absolutist claim that the strength of a right is unyielding culminates in the repudiation of limitation clauses that explicitly authorize the restriction of a constitutional right.[263] In turn, the relativist claim that constitutional rights may be balanced away in their entirety whenever the benefits gained or burdens avoided are sufficiently weighty generates interpretive strain whenever a constitutional provision explicitly guarantees that the core or essence of a constitutional right is immune from incursion. The system of rights does not join the absolutist and relativist models in disregarding constitutional provisions that speak to the strength of rights. On the one hand, the system of rights accommodates limitation clauses by maintaining that when members of the system of rights stand in contextual conflict, justified limitations are possible. On the other hand, the system of rights accommodates provisions that protect the core or essence of rights by explaining why the negation of any member of the system of rights is necessarily unjustifiable. In this way, the system of rights alone explains how familiar constitutional provisions engaging the strength of rights can be taken seriously.

5 Conclusion

What justifies judgments about constitutional rights? Constitutional theorists and practitioners typically respond to this question in different ways.

The predominant view among constitutional theorists is that constitutional judgments raise no distinctive moral principles. Constitutional judgments are justified when they are supported by the balance of moral reasons, and unjustified when they are not. Of course, disagreement persists about what is morally desirable, and whether morality should issue its demands to the scope or strength of rights. But there is broad agreement that the task of legal institutions is to bring about some morally desirable outcome that can be fully comprehended and specified apart from rights-based constitutional order. On this view, constitutional judgment is ordinary moral judgment at scale.

Constitutional practitioners often defend the opposing idea that constitutional judgments are justified when they conform to a set of considerations that are

---

[262] Marcic (1968), p. 68.   [263] Finnis (1985), p. 327; Webber (2014), pp. 147–8.

distinctive to rights-based constitutional law. These considerations are formulated in two overarching doctrines that regulate rights-based adjudication: purposive interpretation and proportionality. The former sets out the sequenced set of considerations apposite to judgments that engage the scope of rights, while the latter sets out the sequenced set of considerations apposite to judgments that engage their strength. Together, these doctrines form a method of resolving constitutional complaints that renders public power accountable to rights. This method can be justified in constitutional law's own terms.

Should constitutional judgments appeal to justificatory resources found outside constitutional law or to justificatory resources found within it? This Element argues that the conception that operates from outside constitutional law generates and perpetuates an impasse between competing models of rights that jointly abandon the rule of law, render rights nugatory, and disregard constitutional text. In contrast, the justificatory conception that operates from within rights-based constitutional law avoids each of these difficulties and explains how rights-based constitutional order is what it purports to be: the rule of law's alternative to placing legal subjects at the mercy of their government.

References

Eric M. Adams (2018), Canadian Constitutional Interpretation, in The Fundamental of Statutory Interpretation (Cameron Hutchinson, ed.), 129–146 (Toronto: LexisNexis).

Dawood Ahmed & Elliot W. Bulmer (2014), Limitation Clauses, International Idea Constitution-Building Primer, www.idea.int/publications/catalogue/limitation-clauses.

Robert Alexy (2002), A Theory of Constitutional Rights (Julian Rivers, trans.) (Oxford: Oxford University Press).

Robert Alexy (2003), Constitutional Rights, Balancing, and Rationality, 16:2 Ratio Juris 131.

Robert Alexy (2007), Thirteen Replies, in Law, Rights, and Discourse: The Legal Philosophy of Robert Alexy (George Pavlakos, ed.), 333–366 (Oxford: Hart).

Robert Alexy (2014), Constitutional Rights and Proportionality, 22 Revus 51.

Robert Alexy (2018), Proportionality and Rationality, in Proportionality: New Challenges, New Frontiers (Vicki C. Jackson & Mark Tushnet, eds.), 13–29 (Cambridge: Cambridge University Press).

Robert Alexy (2021), Law's Ideal Dimension (Oxford: Oxford University Press).

Akhil Reed Amar (1992), The Case of the Missing Amendments: R.A.V. v. City of St. Paul, 106 Harv. L. Rev. 124.

Aharon Barak (2005), Purposive Interpretation in Law (Sari Bashi, trans.) (Princeton: Princeton University Press).

Aharon Barak (2007), Proportional Effect: The Israeli Experience, 57 U.T.L.J. 369.

Aharon Barak (2012), Proportionality: Constitutional Rights and Their Limitations (Doron Kalir, trans.) (Cambridge: Cambridge University Press).

Aharon Barak (2018), A Research Agenda for the Future, in Proportionality: New Frontiers, New Challenges (Vicki C. Jackson and Mark Tushnet, eds.) (Cambridge: Cambridge University Press).

David M. Beatty (2004), The Ultimate Rule of Law (Oxford: Oxford University Press).

Jeremy Bentham (1843), Anarchical Fallacies; Being an Examination of the Declarations of Rights Issued during the French Revolution, in The Works of Jeremy Bentham (vol. 2) (John Bowring, ed.), 489–534 (Edinburgh: William Tait).

Jochen von Bernstorff (2016), Proportionality without Balancing: Why Judicial Ad Hoc Balancing Is Unnecessary, in Reasoning Rights: Comparative Judicial

Engagement (Christopher McCrudden Liora Lazarus & Nigel Bowles, eds.), 63–86 (Oxford: Hart).

Heiner Bielefeldt (2020), Limiting Permissible Limitations: How to Preserve the Substance of Religious Freedom, 15 Relig. & Hum. Rts. 3–19.

Ernst-Wolfgang Böckenförde (2016), Constitutional and Political Theory: Selected Writings (Mirjam Künkler & Tine Stein, eds.) (Jim Underwood & Thomas Dunlap, trans.) (Oxford: Oxford University Press).

Jacco Bomhoff (2013), Balancing Constitutional Rights: The Origins and Meanings of Postwar Legal Discourse (Cambridge: Cambridge University Press).

Robert H. Bork (1971), Neutral Principles and Some First Amendment Problems, 47 Ind. L. J. 1.

Maja Brkan (2018), The Concept of Essence of Fundamental Rights in the EU Legal Order: Peeling the Onion to Its Core, 14 Eur. Const. Rev. 332.

Alan Brudner (2009), What Theory of Rights Best Explain the Oakes Test? in The Limitation of Charter Rights: Critical Essays on R. V. Oakes (Grégoire C. N. Webber & Luc Tremblay, eds.), 59–74 (Montreal: Les Editions Themis).

Mauro Cappelletti (1985), The Expanding Role of Judicial Review in Modern Societies, in The Role of Courts in Society (Simon Shetreet, ed.), 79–96 (Dordrecht: Martinus Nijhoff).

Mauro Cappelletti (1986), Repudiating Montesquieu? The Expansion and Legitimacy of "Constitutional Justice", 35 Cath. U. L. Rev. 1.

Cappelletti (1988), The Expanding Role of Judicial Review in Modern Societies, in The Role of Courts in Society (Simon Shetreet, ed.) (Dordrecht: Martinus Nijhoff).

Bruce Chapman (2011), Ernie's Three Worlds, 61:2 U.T.L.J. 179.

Moshe Cohen-Eliya & Iddo Porat (2011), Proportionality and the Culture of Justification, 59 Am. J. Comp. L. 463.

Moshe Cohen-Eliya & Iddo Porat (2018), The Administrative Origins of Constitutional Rights and Global Constitutionalism, in Proportionality: New Frontiers, New Challenges (Vicki C. Jackson & Mark Tushnet, ed.), 103–129 (Cambridge: Cambridge University Press).

René Descartes (2017), Meditations on First Philosophy (John Cottingham, ed.) (Cambridge: Cambridge University Press).

Günter Dürig (1988), An Introduction to the Basic Law of the Federal Republic of Germany, in The Constitution of the Federal Republic of Germany (Ulrich Karpen, ed.), 11–24 (Baden-Baden: Nomos Verlagsgesellschaft).

Ronald Dworkin (1978), Taking Rights Seriously (Cambridge, MA: Harvard University Press).

Ronald Dworkin (1990), A Bill of Rights for Britain (London: Chatto & Windus).
Ronald Dworkin (1996), Objectivity and Truth: You'd Better Believe It, 25:2 Phil. & Pub. Aff. 87.
Ronald Dworkin (2006), Is Democracy Possible Here? Principles for a New Debate (Princeton: Princeton University Press).
Ronald Dworkin (2011), Justice for Hedgehogs (Cambridge, MA: Belknap Press of the Harvard University Press).
Dan Edelstein (2018), On the Spirit of Rights (Chicago: University of Chicago Press).
John Hart Ely (1980), Democracy and Distrust (Cambridge, MA: Harvard University Press).
Christopher Essert (2024), Property Law in the Society of Equals (Oxford: Oxford University Press).
Colin Feasby (2022), The Evolving Approach to Charter Interpretation, 60:1 Alb. L. Rev. 35.
John Finnis (1972), Some Professorial Fallacies about Rights, 4 Adel. L. Rev. 377.
John Finnis (1980), Natural Law and Natural Rights (Oxford: Oxford University Press).
John Finnis (1985), A Bill of Rights for Britain? The Moral of Contemporary Jurisprudence, 71 Proc. Brit. Ac. 303.
John Finnis (1994), Law, Morality, and "Sexual Orientation," 69 Notre Dame L. Rev. 1049.
John Finnis (2013), A Response to Harel, Hope, and Schwartz, 8 Jrslm Rev. Legal Stud. 147.
John Finnis (2015), Grounding Human Rights in Natural Law, 60 Am. J. Juris. 199.
Stanley Fish (2008), Intention Is all There Is: A Critical Analysis of Aharon Barak's Purposive Interpretation in Law, 29:3 Cardozo L. Rev. 1109.
James E. Fleming (2004), Securing Deliberative Democracy, 72 Fordham L. Rev. 1435.
Laurent B. Frantz (1962), The First Amendment in the Balance, 71 Yale L. J. 1424.
Danny Frederick (2014), Pro-Tanto Versus Absolute Rights, 45 Phil. Forum 375.
Oscar M. Garibaldi (1976), General Limitations on Human Rights: The Principle of Legality, 17 Harv. Int'l L. J. 503.
Stephen Gardbaum (2014), Proportionality and Democratic Constitutionalism, in Proportionality and the Rule of Law: Rights, Justification, Reasoning (Grant Huscroft, Bradley W. Miller, & Grégoire Webber, eds.), 259–283 (Cambridge: Cambridge University Press).
Jamal Greene (2018), Foreword: Rights as Trumps, 132 Harv. L. Rev. 28.
Jamal Greene (2021), How Rights Went Wrong (New York: HarperCollins).

Dieter Grimm (1994), Human Rights and Judicial Review in Germany, in Human Rights and Judicial Review: A Comparative Perspective (David Beatty, ed.), 277–295 (Dordrecht: Martinus Nijhoff).

Dieter Grimm (2007), Proportionality in Canadian and German Constitutional Jurisprudence, 57 UTLJ 383.

Dieter Grimm (2009), Freedom of Speech in a Globalized World, in Extreme Speech and Democracy (Ivan Hare and James Weinstein, eds.) (Oxford: Oxford University Press).

Dieter Grimm (2010), The Basic Law at 60 – Identity and Change, 11 German L. J. 33.

Dieter Grimm (2015), The Role of Fundamental Rights after Sixty-Five Years of Constitutional Jurisprudence in Germany, 13 Int'l J. Const. L. 9.

Dieter Grimm (2016), Constitutionalism: Past, Present, and Future (Oxford: Oxford University Press).

Dieter Grimm (2019), What Exactly Is Political about Constitutional Adjudication? in Judicial Power: How Constitutional Courts Affect Political Transformations (Christine Landfried, ed.), 307–317 (Cambridge: Cambridge University Press).

Dieter Grimm (2020), Dieter Grimm: Advocate of the Constitution (Justin Collings, trans.) (Oxford: Oxford University Press).

Jürgen Habermas (1996), Between Facts and Norms: Contributions to a Discourse Theory of Democracy (William Rehg, trans.) (Cambridge, MA: MIT Press).

Peter W. Hogg (2007), Constitutional Law of Canada (vol. 2) (Toronto: Thomson Carswell).

John P. Humphrey (1979), The Just Requirements of Morality, Public Order, and the General Welfare in a Democratic Society, in The Practice of Freedom (R. St. J. Macdonald & John P. Humphrey, eds.), 137–156 (Toronto: Butterworths).

Frank Iacobucci (2003), Reconciling Rights: The Supreme Court of Canada's Approach to Competing Charter Rights, 20 Sup. C. L. Rev. 137.

Walter Jellinek (1946), Grundrechte und Gesetzesvorbehalt, 1 Deutsche Rechts-Zeitschrift 4.

Alexandre Charles Kiss (1981), Permissible Limitations on Rights, in The International Bill of Rights: The Covenant on Civil and Political Rights (Louis Henkin, ed.), 290–310 (New York: Columbia University Press).

Matthias Klatt (2014), An Egalitarian Defense of Proportionality-Based Balancing: A Reply to Luc B. Tremblay, 12 Int'l J. Const. L. 891.

Matthias Klatt & Moritz Meister (2012), The Constitutional Structure of Proportionality (Oxford: Oxford University Press).

Mattias Kumm (2007), Political Liberalism and the Structure of Rights: On the Place and Limits of Proportionality Requirement, in Law, Rights, and Discourse: The Legal Philosophy of Robert Alexy (George Pavlakos, ed.), 131–166 (Oxford: Hart).

Mattias Kumm (2010), The Idea of Socratic Contestation and the Right to Justification: The Point of Rights-Based Proportionality Review, 4 Law & Ethics Hum. Rts. 142.

Mattias Kumm (2018), Is the Structure of Human Rights Practice Defensible? Three Puzzles and Their Solution, in Proportionality: New Frontiers, New Challenges (Vicki C. Jackson & Mark Tushnet, ed.), 51–74 (Cambridge: Cambridge University Press).

Dimitrios Kyritsis (2014), Whatever Works: Proportionality as a Constitutional Doctrine, 34 Oxford J. Legal Stud. 395.

Ingrid Leijten (2018), Core Socio-Economic Rights and the European Court of Human Rights (Cambridge: Cambridge University Press).

Koen Lenaerts (2019), Limits on Limitations: The Essence of Fundamental Rights in the EU, 20 German L. J. 779.

George Letsas (2007), A Theory of Interpretation of the European Convention on Human Rights (Oxford: Oxford University Press).

Thilo Marauhn & Nadine Ruppel (2008), Balancing Conflicting Rights: Konrad Hesse's Notion of "Praktische Konkordanz" and the German Federal Constitutional Court, in Conflicts between Fundamental Rights (Eva Brems, ed.), 273–296 (Antwerp: Intersentia).

René Marcic (1968), Duties and Limitations upon Rights, 9 Int'l Comm. Jur. Rev. 59.

Karl Marx (2010), The Constitution of the French Republic Adopted November 4, 1848, in Marx & Engels: Collected Works (vol. 10) (Anna Vladimirova and Lyudgarda Zubrilova, eds.), 567–580 (London: Lawrence & Wishart).

Alexander Meiklejohn (1961), The First Amendment Is an Absolute, Sup. Ct. Rev. 245.

Bradley W. Miller (2008), Justification and Rights Limitation, in Expounding the Constituion: Essays in Constitutional Theory (Grant Huscroft, ed.) (Cambridge: Cambridge University Press).

Kai Möller (2012a), The Global Model of Constitutional Rights (Oxford: Oxford University Press).

Kai Möller (2012b), Proportionality: Challenging the Critics, 10 Int'l J. Const. L. 709.

Kai Möller (2014), Proportionality and Rights Inflation, in Proportionality and the Rule of Law: Rights, Justification, Reasoning (Grant Huscroft, Bradley

W. Miller, & Grégoire Webber, eds.), 155–172 (Cambridge: Cambridge University Press).

Kai Möller (2018), US Constitutional Law, Proportionality, and the Global Model, in Proportionality: New Challenges, New Frontiers (Vicki C. Jackson & Mark Tushnet, eds.), 130–147 (Cambridge: Cambridge University Press).

Phillip Montague (2001), When Rights Conflict, 7 Legal Theory 257.

Ettienne Mureinik (1994), A Bridge to Where – Introducing the Interim Bill of Rights, 10 South Afr. J. Hum. Rts. 31.

John Oberdiek (2008), Specifying Rights Out of Necessity, 28 Oxford J. Legal Stud. 127.

John Oberdiek (2010), Specifying Constitutional Rights, 27 Const. Commentary 231.

Esin Örücü (1986), The Core of Rights and Freedoms: The Limits of Limits, in Human Rights: From Rhetoric to Reality (Tom Campbell, ed.), 37–51 (New York: Blackwell).

Thomas Paine (1992), The Rights of Man (Gregory Claeys, ed.) (Indianapolis: Hackett).

Ralf Poscher (2021), Proportionality and the Bindingness of Fundamental Rights, in Proportionality in Crime Control and Criminal Justice (Emmanouil Billis, Nandor Knust, & Jon Petter Rui, eds.), 49–68 (Oxford: Hart).

Neomi Rao (2008), On the Use and Abuse of Dignity in Constitutional Law, 14 Colum. J. Eur. L. 201.

John Rawls (1999), A Theory of Justice: Revised Edition (Cambridge, MA: Belknap Press).

Arthur Ripstein (2007), Anti-Archimedeanism, in Ronald Dworkin (Arthur Ripstein, ed.), 1–21 (Cambridge: Cambridge University Press).

Arthur Ripstein (2021), Kant and the Laws of War (Oxford: Oxford University Press).

Julian Rivers (2006), Proportionality and Variable Intensity of Review, 65 Cambridge L. J. 174.

Julian Rivers (2012), Constitutional Rights and Statutory Limitations, in Institutionalized Reason: The Jurisprudence of Robert Alexy (Matthias Klatt, ed.), 248–272 (Oxford: Oxford University Press).

William David Ross (1930), The Right and the Good (Philip Straton-Lake, ed.) (Oxford: Oxford University Press).

Russ Schafer-Landau (1995), Specifying Absolute Rights, 37 Ariz. L. Rev. 209.

Marcus Schladebach (2014), Praktische Konkordanz Als Verfassungsrechtliches Kollisionprinzip: Eine Verteidigung, 53 Der Staat 263.

Steven D. Smith (1994), Moral Realism, Pluralistic Community, and the Judicial Imposition of Principle: A Comment on Perry, 88:1 Nw. U. L. Rev. 183.

References

Carl Schmitt (2005), Political Theology: Four Chapters on the Concept of Sovereignty (George Schwab, trans.) (Chicago: University of Chicago Press).

Martin Stone (2011), Legal Positivism as an Idea about Morality, 61 U.T.L.J. 313.

Martin Stone (2012), Planning Positivism and Natural Law, 25 Can. J.L. & Jur. 219.

Alex Stone Sweet and Jud Mathews (2019), Proportionality Balancing and Constitutional Governance: A Comparative and Global Approach (Oxford: Oxford University Press).

Gerald Stourzh (2021), Democratic Participation and Human Rights Protection as a System of Equal Rights (Chicago: University of Chicago Press).

Peter Strawson (1992), Analysis and Metaphysics: An Introduction to Philosophy (New York: Oxford University Press).

Judith Jarvis Thomson (1986), Self-Defense and Rights, in Rights, Restitution, and Risk: Essays in Moral Theory (William Parent, ed.), 33–48 (Cambridge: Harvard University Press).

Malcolm Thorburn (2016), Proportionality, in Philosophical Foundations of Constitutional Law (David Dyzenhaus & Malcolm Thorburn, eds.), 305–322 (Oxford: Oxford University Press).

Luc B. Tremblay (2014), An Egalitarian Defense of Proportionality-Based Balancing, 12 Int'l J Const. L. 864.

Luc B. Tremblay (2015), An Egalitarian Defense of Proportionality-Based Balancing, 12 Int'l J. Const. L. 900.

Stavros Tsakyrakis (2009), Proportionality: An Assault on Human Rights, 7 Int'l J. Const. L. 468.

William Twining (1975), The Contemporary Significance of Bentham's Anarchical Fallacies, 61 ARSP 325.

Francisco J. Urbina (2017), A Critique of Balancing and Proportionality (Cambridge: Cambridge University Press).

Jeremy Waldron (1999), Law and Disagreement (Oxford: Oxford University Press).

Mark Walters (2020), A.V. Dicey and the Common Law Constitutional Tradition: A Legal Turn of Mind (Cambridge: Cambridge University Press).

Grégoire Webber (2012), The Negotiable Constitution: On the Limitation of Rights (Cambridge: Cambridge University Press).

Grégoire Webber (2013), Rights and the Rule of Law in the Balance, 129 Law Q. Rev. 399.

Grégoire Webber (2014), On the Loss of Rights, in Proportionality and the Rule of Law: Rights, Justification, Reasoning (Grant Huscroft, Bradley W. Miller, & Grégoire Webber, eds.), 123–154 (Cambridge: Cambridge University Press).

References

Grégoire Webber & Paul Yowell (2018), Introduction, in Legislated Rights: Securing Human Rights Through Legislation, 1–26 (Cambridge: Cambridge University Press).

Ernest J. Weinrib (1995), The Idea of Private Law (Cambridge, MA: Harvard University Press).

Jacob Weinrib (2016), Dimensions of Dignity: The Theory and Practice of Modern Constitutional Law (Cambridge: Cambridge University Press).

Jacob Weinrib (2017), When Trumps Clash: Dworkin and the Doctrine of Proportionality, 30 Ratio Juris 341.

Jacob Weinrib (forthcoming 2025), The Essence of Rights and the Limits of Proportionality, in The Promise of Legality: Critical Reflections upon the Work of T.R.S. Allan (Geneviève Cartier & Mark Walters, eds.) (Oxford: Hart Publishing).

Jacob Weinrib (2024), What Is Purposive Interpretation? 74:1 U.T.L.J. 74.

Lorraine E. Weinrib (2002), Canada's Charter of Rights: Paradigm Lost? 6 Rev. Const Stud. 119.

Christopher Heath Wellman (1995), On Conflicts between Rights, 14 Law & Phil. 271.

Lorenzo Zucca (2007), Constitutional Dilemmas: Conflicts of Fundamental Legal Rights in Europe (Oxford: Oxford University Press).

Ariel Zylberman (2022), Moral Rights without Balancing, 179 Phil. Stud. 549a.

Acknowledgements

I am deeply grateful to everyone who contributed to this project. For helpful conversations and comments, I would like to thank Eric M. Adams, Trevor Allan, Aharon Barak, Ilana Bleichert, Ian Davis, Hassan Dindjer, Chris Essert, Colin Feasby, Colleen M. Flood, Colin Grey, Alon Harel, Jeff King, Howie Kislowicz, Mattias Kumm, Rory Gillis, Dieter Grimm, Glenn Joyal, Joanna Langille, George Letsas, Ryan Liss, Vanessa MacDonnell, Margaret Martin, Carissima Mathen, Melanie Maurer, Peter Oliver, Manish Oza, Zoltán Pozsár-Szentmiklósy, Akis Psygkas, Amnon Reichman, Arthur Ripstein, Zoë Sinel, Terry Skolnik, Martin Stone, Malcolm Thorburn, Mark Walters, Grégoire Webber, Rivka Weill, Lael Weis, James S. F. Wilson, Andy Yu, Ariel Zylberman, and two anonymous referees for Cambridge University Press. I am also indebted to the editors of this series for their support and patience: Sally Zhu, Kenneth M. Ehrenberg, Gerald J. Postema, and George Pavlakos. Finally, thanks is due to Krithika Shivakumar.

I am fortunate to have worked with extraordinarily talented research assistants throughout this project. Oliver Flis and Abigail Bergeron wrote illuminating and perceptive research memos. Hannah Colbert and Benjamin Zolf provided excellent editorial assistance. Megan Pfiffer edited the entire manuscript with tremendous skill and insight. This project was supported by an Insight Development Grant from the Social Science and Humanities Research Council of Canada.

I am profoundly indebted to the hundreds of Queen's Law students who braved my constitutional law courses, and whose thoughtful questions and comments over the years propelled me deeper and deeper into the ideas in this Element. In particular, I owe a debt of gratitude to the law and philosophy students in my 2023 Jurisprudence seminar, who workshopped an earlier version of this Element. I am so lucky to have routinely encountered such remarkable students.

Most of all, I am indebted to the love and support of my family: to my parents, Ernest and Lorraine Weinrib, who taught me – among many other things – legal theory and comparative constitutional law, respectively; to my wife, Debra Hamer; and our remarkable children, Max and Reuben.

To Maya, Hannah, Leila, Max, Reuben, and their generation

Cambridge Elements⁼

Philosophy of Law

Series Editors
George Pavlakos
University of Glasgow

George Pavlakos is Professor of Law and Philosophy at the School of Law, University of Glasgow. He has held visiting posts at the universities of Kiel and Luzern, the European University Institute, the UCLA Law School, the Cornell Law School and the Beihang Law School in Beijing. He is the author of *Our Knowledge of the Law* (2007) and more recently has co-edited *Agency, Negligence and Responsibility* (2021) and *Reasons and Intentions in Law and Practical Agency* (2015).

Gerald J. Postema
University of North Carolina at Chapel Hill

Gerald J. Postema is Professor Emeritus of Philosophy at the University of North Carolina at Chapel Hill. Among his publications count *Utility, Publicity, and Law: Bentham's Moral and Legal Philosophy* (2019); *On the Law of Nature, Reason, and the Common Law: Selected Jurisprudential Writings of Sir Matthew Hale* (2017); *Legal Philosophy in the Twentieth Century: The Common Law World* (2011), *Bentham and the Common Law Tradition*, 2nd edition (2019).

Kenneth M. Ehrenberg
University of Surrey

Kenneth M. Ehrenberg is Professor of Jurisprudence and Philosophy at the University of Surrey School of Law and Co-Director of the Surrey Centre for Law and Philosophy. He is the author of *The Functions of Law* (2016) and numerous articles on the nature of law, jurisprudential methodology, the relation of law to morality, practical authority, and the epistemology of evidence law.

Associate Editor
Sally Zhu
University of Sheffield

Sally Zhu is a Lecturer in Property Law at University of Sheffield. Her research is on property and private law aspects of platform and digital economies.

About the Series

This series provides an accessible overview of the philosophy of law, drawing on its varied intellectual traditions in order to showcase the interdisciplinary dimensions of jurisprudential enquiry, review the state of the art in the field, and suggest fresh research agendas for the future. Focussing on issues rather than traditions or authors, each contribution seeks to deepen our understanding of the foundations of the law, ultimately with a view to offering practical insights into some of the major challenges of our age.

Cambridge Elements

Philosophy of Law

Elements in the Series

Revisiting the Rule of Law
Kristen Rundle

The Place of Coercion in Law
Triantafyllos Gkouvas

The Differentiation and Autonomy of Law
Emilios Christodoulidis

The Moral Prerequisites of the Criminal Law: Legal Moralism and the Problem of Mala Prohibita
Ambrose Y. K. Lee and Alexander F. Sarch

Legal Personhood
Visa A. J. Kurki

The Philosophy of Legal Proof
Lewis Ross

The Normativity of Law
Michael Giudice

Legal Rights and Moral Rights
Matthew H. Kramer

Dignity and Rights
Ariel Zylberman

Subsidiarity
Andreas Follesdal

Contemporary Non-Positivism
Emad H. Atiq

The Impasse of Constitutional Rights
Jacob Weinrib

A full series listing is available at: www.cambridge.org/EPHL

For EU product safety concerns, contact us at Calle de José Abascal, 56–1°,
28003 Madrid, Spain or eugpsr@cambridge.org.